SINKING SAND, SOLID ROCK

MARSHALL PRYOR

CONTENTS

To my wonderful, patient, loving family:
Carole, Curtis, Jana, Demetre, and Michael

Acknowledgments

I told God I could not have completed this book without His help, so He introduced me to a marvelous friend and book consultant named JP Mark. Thank you, JP, for your knowledge, wisdom, and guidance. My friend and computer consultant, Owen Mark, has been a marvelous help in leading me through the maze of "high tech" computer needs. Christi Martin, my editor and proofreader, has reviewed many of my draft copies and made needed changes to comply with proper English and my Texas slanguage. Thank you also to Amber Helt of Rooted in Writing, my talented book designer, and Rashmita Paul, my cover artist.

Several individuals graciously stepped up and agreed to review manuscript versions of this book, and I am grateful to each of them. Thank you, Jim Applegate, Lanny Snodgrass, P. D. James, A. Dwight Burchett, Stan Houts, Ben Catlin, Bruce Crawford, and David Siegel for your comments, suggestions, and corrections. Of course, any errors that remain are entirely my own.

Thank you also to the people who have been vital in my life's journey and who are an integral part of this book: Curtis Smith, my mentor and guide along the way; my seminary professors Dr. Taylor,

Dr. Grider, Dr. Purkiser, and Dr. McGraw; and the faithful church laypeople, more than I have room to name—may the Great God of heaven bless you and place His everlasting arms around you.

To those who patiently listened while I tried my best to preach the Word, may God bless you to the utmost.

My deep desire and hope is that I shall never fail in my duty, but that at all times, and especially right now, I shall be full of courage, so that with my whole being I shall bring honor to Christ, whether I live or die.

— Philippians 1:20 GNT

Preface

Every day I am alive is a gift from God. Considering the number of times I've come close to death, I believe God gave me life and sustained me on earth for a higher purpose, perhaps to help others by sharing my story, my knowledge, and maybe even some hard-earned wisdom.

Some people may decide my life's story is just a series of random events, some good and some bad, and that overall, Marshall Pryor was one of the lucky ones—a survivor. Maybe so. I have no hidden agenda and no desire to foist my ideas or testimony on anyone who doesn't want them.

I came into this world with the advantage of devoted and caring parents who loved God and taught me right from wrong, but I also had some significant disadvantages, mostly physical. Because of a medical condition, I was uncommonly small throughout my early years. Up until the age of seventeen, I was scarcely bigger than a dwarf and grew no taller than four feet, eleven inches. I was also born with a deviated septum that extruded from my nose, a disfigurement that led some people, mostly other children, to mock and insult me. The feeling of being "less than" in my early life was constant and unyielding. On top of that, I seemed to attract lethal danger at every turn and barely made it through childhood.

The first time I nearly died was in 1939. I was six months old. My mama wanted a cute picture of me on the back of our horse. For no reason, the horse got spooked and kicked up a little. Not a huge buck, but just enough to send me head over heels off its back. As I fell, the horse gave me a swift, hard kick to my stomach and ruptured the inner wall of my abdomen. The accident well-nigh killed me right then and there. No operation for an accident of that type existed in those days, but I finally had surgery in the eighth grade. For twelve years, I was forced to wear a truss around my abdomen twenty-four hours a day, because my body could not heal on its own. The risk of death loomed over me constantly. I don't remember the incident, but I vividly remember wearing the truss with a rather soft, rubbery ball sewn into the lining to force pressure on my guts. The sensation never leaves me.

The next time death hovered, I was only three years old. Shortly after the Great Depression, my family lived in Cisco, Texas. World War II had just started, but most men who lived there were still without work. The Depression hit Texas harder than most places. Hundreds rode the rails through Cisco—hobos, bums, the desperate, and the discouraged. Almost as many foolhardy and dangerous men lived in our small town as permanent residents. One sunny, warm spring day, I was playing alone in my backyard when, for whatever reason, I followed a squirrel and wandered off. My dad was a preacher in Cisco, and my mom turned her back for a minute to look after my older sister. When she looked again, I was gone.

My parents became frantic—sobbing and calling friends, relatives, and neighbors. Their three-year-old son disappeared. Soon the entire community was alerted, searching in old iceboxes, under houses, and down by the railroad where all the drifters and tramps cussed and smoked cigarettes. Some of them were mean, but most were simply lost in hopelessness, going from east to west and west to east to find work, or anything. Did one of those drifters kidnap the little Cisco boy? Oh, the horrible thoughts going through the minds of those uncomplicated Texas people, church people, family folks.

I sat unharmed between the tracks of the railroad in the midst of danger! I had no idea how close I was to death. Was God there? Were the angels? I don't know. I don't have one of those TV stories about a little kid protected by aliens. This I do know: through the mercy and grace of God, a few hours later, I was found.

My sense of security was short-lived. Three years later, when I was six, my family went on a camping trip along the Rio Grande River, and another incident occurred that had a lasting impact on the rest of my life. As I strolled along the riverbed, I didn't notice a patch of sinking sand. My feet sank deep into a pit, and I hollered. I was fortunate to be small and light, but sink I did. In a blink, the sand was up to my chest.

Luckily, my daddy and a friend heard my screams and came running. Many terrifying minutes later, I was rescued, but that incident deeply influenced how I saw the world. From that moment onward, I knew solid ground was an illusion, and death could happen in the blink of an eye. My nightmares ended only after many years; my mind constantly relived that frightening moment when the earth swallowed me up like Korah's people in Numbers 16. I eventually learned to trust only God who, through His grace, protected and defended me.

Fast forward to about 1953 in the desert hills outside Carlsbad, New Mexico. Teenagers, high school kids exploring, having fun. High on a rugged hill, a small stream of water dropped from the top, falling about a hundred feet to a small pool below and then on to another rocky, desert stream. Wanting to find where the water was coming from, I ran to the top where it was bubbling out of the ground and followed the small stream as it washed over the rocks, leaving behind slick green moss.

Once again, just like my three-year-old self, curiosity took over my immature mind, and I decided I had to see what was beyond the next hill. I slid on the moss as though it was a giant roller coaster. Down I went on slippery moss, around a boulder. Laughing, I was lifted to a small contour in the rocks and pushed onward. I couldn't stop! No more than two or three feet ahead of me, the ground dropped at least a hundred feet. Suddenly something, or Someone, stopped me from certain death. As water swirled around me and tumbled below, I peered over the frightening cliff, scared out of my mind.

What if I moved? How could I move? Who stopped me? An angel? God?

How could I emerge unscathed so many times from such accidents that put me face-to-face with death?

A few years ago, I went back to Cisco and visited the old home-place ranch. The smokehouse was abandoned, as was the cistern, cellar, and barn. The place was like a cemetery of the forsaken. Everything else at the old homeplace had been torn down. But strangely, I felt a presence. Memories, I guess. But memories alone are just, well, memories. This feeling was more—more like an experience. I searched for answers and, instead, at the place where my earliest memories began, I found God in a new way.

Gathered around the old woodstove, praying in the front room, Daddy and Grandpa talked to the Lord. More than that, they experienced God as they prayed. We knew it! I knew it too as I stepped around the broken wooden pieces of the torn-down ranch house way out in Texas country north of Cisco.

A bull or two mingled with the few cows that came to inspect the stranger invading their territory, hoping for some cow-cake. I didn't care; I was lost in the recollection of our family Bible reading and Spirit-filled prayer. My grandpa and daddy and mama could really pray. They prayed, heaven came down, and glory touched my soul. Does anyone know how to pray anymore in the way that brings heaven and earth together?

PART I

FAITH QUESTIONS

1

Cisco, Texas

Innocence is the beauty and joy of the child.

The first three years of life are crucial in the development of learning, giving, affection, trust, and mental stimulation. Love is essential to a child's brain architecture, and fortunately, my parents gave me that. My small-town experience of Cisco in north-central Texas was one like no other—family, simplicity, love, church, horses, blacksmiths, cattle, laughter.

If you draw a line from east to west across the United States from southern California to South Carolina, Cisco would be smack-dab in the middle, more than twelve hundred miles from each coast. The place was the temporary home to so many vagrants, drifters, and journeymen—not to mention oil workers—that it turned out to be the perfect spot for a hotel. According to Archbridge Institute's article, "Conrad Hilton: The Dreamer Who Conquered an Industry," an entrepreneur named Conrad Hilton started his empire in Cisco, Texas, in 1919 when he managed to buy the three-year-old, forty-room Mobley Hotel from Henry Mobley for $40,000 (about $600,000 in 2020) and discovered it was a veritable gold mine. Mobley sold out to Hilton, thinking that the big money opportunity was in oil, not a "glorified boardinghouse," but Mobley was wrong. Rooms at the hotel turned over three times a day to oil workers who stayed in each room in eight-hour shifts.

Buying the Mobley in Cisco may have been a lucky accident for Hilton, but it proved to be the tiny seed that sprouted and grew his business into a hotel behemoth. In 1946, nearly thirty years later, Hilton promised his then eighty-five-year-old mother to buy her the biggest hotel in the world. Sure enough, though she didn't live long enough to see him accomplish it, he acquired the management rights to the Waldorf Astoria Hotel in New York City on October 12, 1949, and bought the hotel outright in 1972.

As for the humble Mobley, Hilton sold it ten years later in 1929 to free up cash for his other hotel investments, and the hotel went to ruin during the Depression. In 1977, the Hilton family purchased the property and donated it to the University of Houston Foundation. Today, more than a hundred years later, anyone can visit Hilton's first hotel in Cisco, which is now a refurbished tourist attraction, community center, museum, and city park.

To this day, the high-water mark for Cisco's population was in 1920, at nearly 7,500 residents. Nowadays, we might believe it a disadvantage to live in a place like Cisco and not a big city like Dallas or Chicago, but just the opposite is true. Besides its connection to the founding of the Hilton hotel empire, over the decades, Cisco proved to be fertile ground for a number of notable people, including Dan and Farris Wilks, the billionaire brothers who invented the hydraulic fracturing that revolutionized the petroleum industry, and Dash Crofts, who found fame and fortune in the 1970s as part of the soft-rock duo Seals and Crofts. Although it was a small community, Cisco had the advantages of extremely strong church and family ties, something many city dwellers don't fully appreciate. And the fact that a Conrad Hilton could start a hotel empire in such a humble location as Cisco gave everyone there, myself included, a small boost of confidence to believe that doing big things in life was possible.

Back in the 1800s, pioneers came through and stayed in that part of Texas. Among them were the Parmers who brought with them farming and ranching skills . . . and a bunch of pigs, many of which escaped and became feral. That's why so many wild pigs live in Texas—blame it on the Parmers.

My mama was a Parmer. Her family settled in Jack County and Eastland County. Some of the Parmers went south to neighboring Comanche County to find wives there. I am told I am at least part Comanche. One of the early Parmers, Martin Parmer, was an original signer of the Texas Constitution, and his son, Toby, my great grandpa, was one of the first Texas Rangers.

Some of the Parmers went to the south side of Eastland County to a little town just north of Comanche County called Rising Star. There, the Andrew, Agnew, Buckner, and Messegee families had a whole lot of kids and intermarried with only God knows who. Great Grandpa Parmer, Toby, married Mary Jane Buckner in 1861. She was born July 8, 1843, and died May 20, 1919. Together they had a caboodle of kids named William Lafayette (Uncle Will), Sarah (she lived to be 103), Eliza, Angelina, Martin Van Buren Jr. (my grandpa, they called him Uncle Van, born February 8, 1871, and died September 10, 1965), George, and Myrtle.

The Civil War shook Texas up. People from back east and over in Europe began pouring into Texas by the hundreds and thousands and took over Comanche land. My relatives said the Comanches were vicious, murdering terrorists who ventured as far south as Mexico to kill people down there. My family believed Native Americans would have killed each other had the white people not given them a common enemy. They said the Native Americans killed each other by the thousands, destroyed their environment, and left mayhem everywhere they went. It's not appropriate to say any of that now. The real truth lies somewhere hidden in the past.

According to Grandpa Parmer, the Comanches lived all through the Cisco, Texas area. He ought to have known, because his daddy, my great grandpa Toby, married a part Comanche. Their sons, Will and Van, did too. Uncle Will and Grandpa Van married two Comanche sisters from Rising Star, Texas. The Rising Star sisters didn't have a Comanche surname like Paraiboo—theirs was Agnew. The early settlers cared little where their spouses came from because Texas was big, and they needed lots of kids to work the land.

Great Grandma was home alone with Grandpa Van when he was a baby. All the rest of the family worked in the field. According to family history, a bunch of Comanches surrounded the ranch house on their horses, and one guy jumped on the porch, trying to get in. My great grandma took a shotgun and killed him as the Comanche came through the door. If you saw her picture, she looks like she wouldn't need a gun to kill anyone. The other Indians left when this happened. I don't know if my family buried the Indian or not, or when. Maybe his remains are still there under the porch.

All through Texas during the mid-1800s, there were buffalo, panthers, turkeys, bobcats, otters, armadillos, and birds of every kind, including whooping cranes and prairie chickens. Grandpa Parmer used to tell me about how both his family and the Comanches hunted together after peace was signed and after the Civil War. A great many buffalo roamed in that part of Texas, but those buffalo skedaddled north, 'cause they knew if they stayed, they'd be killed. It turned out not to matter, because "Buffalo Bill" Cody killed them anyway.

The Comanches killed them with arrows and spears, many times leaving them lying there after they took what they needed. No iceboxes existed in Cisco at that time.

The Battle of the Alamo, which was a mission in San Antonio, ushered Texas into a decidedly different culture, along with the Mexican-American War of 1846. Pioneers by the hundreds started moving into Texas, but that didn't immediately stop the Comanches from continuing to protect their land. Gradually, people intermarried—Mexicans, Comanches, and whites.

Uncle Will was older than Grandpa Van and settled with his part-Comanche wife not far outside the town of Cisco, going west toward Putnam and Abilene. People of the town said Uncle Will had more money than anybody, and when his wife died, he married another woman who was kinda mean. The rumor was that she killed Uncle Will, but there was no proof. I remember sitting in the living room with his body at a three-day wake. People made like they were crying, but it seemed like a show to me. After that, they ate. I liked to go into the kitchen and grab stuff when no one was looking. Nobody drank fire-water, even at funerals, because it was bad, and besides, Eastland County was a dry county. The Methodist Episcopal Church South, Nazarene, Southern Baptist, and Campbellite Church of Christ churches ruled the roost, and back in those days, none of them drank anything with alcohol. By the way, the Southern Baptists wouldn't be caught dead with other church people, especially Campbellites. No Catholics and Episcopalians lived there, as they drank everything.

When Grandpa was born, Cisco was barely a town. It first became a real place when a traveling preacher put roots down and let people know he was starting a church. The Methodist Episcopal Church South folks were first, then came the Baptists, and then the Campbellites, named after Thomas Campbell, a Presbyterian minister (later known as the Disciples of Christ and Church of Christ—they didn't believe in musical instruments in church). The Church of Christ people started a college in Abilene, and that's where the singer Pat Boone got his start. The Nazarenes didn't come along until later, about 1906 or 1908, so I guess the first shall be last and the last first. Nazarenes were the only really saved people. (Just joking!)

When Grandpa Van got older, he found and married his part-Comanche wife from Rising Star. Her name was Carrie. Grandpa and Grandma settled way out north of Cisco on a section of land suitable for farming and grazing cattle but not much else. At the time, Cisco had less than a thousand people, but do you know what? Back in those days, ranchers from Texas drove over three million (that's right, folks) cows (and bulls too) all the way up to Abilene, Kansas!

By the time Grandpa had his ranch, he had taken some of them to Armour Packing Company in Fort Worth. All the cows were

Hereford—red and white-faced. Armour Packing Company had a redheaded goat that lived in the cow lot, appropriately named Judas. A long, narrow chute went from the cow lot up about two to three stories high, probably twenty to thirty feet. The cows hated to go up, so Judas would start toward the chute while the ranch hands gently herded them toward the goat. As Judas walked up the chute, the cows followed—slick as a whistle. When they got to the top, old Judas moved off to the side, and the workers hit the cows right in the middle of the head and killed them. Then they pulled the dead cows by the legs and cut 'em open so people could eat 'em.

Fortunately, the oil company struck oil and then natural gas in and around Cisco. Grandpa had several oil and gas wells. Lone Star Gas Company came by now and then and got the gas or turned some wheels and sent it to the refinery. Grandpa could use some of it to put in his old car. Since it was unrefined, it blew black smoke to kingdom come. All this made him a rich man, but no one knew what rich meant, and nobody cared anyway.

Every night Grandpa would listen to radio preachers by putting his ear real close to the sound and turning up the radio all the way, so loud that all of us had to go into the kitchen. It hurt our ears. Unfortunately, Grandpa donated a great deal of money to a radio evangelist named Dan Gilbert of Upland, "Caleefarnya," to get Bibles to people in jail. Daddy said it was about $63,000 back in the 1950s—that's more than half a million dollars today. Grandpa really wanted to help prisoners get Bibles.

Grandpa listened to ol' Dannyboy Gilbert over the Del Rio, Texas radio station. His radio was powered by a car battery and kept charged by the wind outside. The wind charger was kinda like those big ones out in the deserts of California but smaller. Grandpa's heart was right, but ol' Dannyboy was a crook holding himself out as a preacher of sorts. He was into gettin' chained down by hookers and was found dead in a sleazy motel somewhere close to Los Angeles, killed by the husband of his pregnant mistress. Grandpa gave a lot of money to the Nazarene Church, too—and to the Methodist Episcopal Church South.

Later on, Daddy became the young pastor of the Nazarene Church in Cisco when the Great Santa Claus Bank Robbery took place in 1927.

It's written in history books, and Daddy told me all about it. One of the robbers dressed up like Santa Claus, which made it perfect because it was close to Christmas. It seemed like people had a kind of innocence about them, especially in small towns, so this robber, "Santa," walked down the street, making everybody happy. His other bad guys were waiting around while he went into the bank. In today's dollars, they got over $2 million. Outside of town, a couple of good ol' Texas boys with guns shot one of the robbers in the arm—or someplace—and caused them to hightail it out of town. It produced one of the largest manhunts in Texas even to this day.

Members of the posse that went after the robbers.

Unfortunately, the Santa Claus robber killed the police chief. Since it was Christmastime, on the following Sunday, a church member dressed up as Santa and entered the service. A little boy in the church was scared and yelled out, "Santa Claus, why did you rob our bank?"

When Grandma died, Grandpa started giving all eight of his kids, and my mom, a thousand dollars each Christmas. Uncle Earl passed away from carbuncles, and "Aunt" Tince's mother got killed by lightning when Tince was just a baby. Her daddy couldn't take care of her, so she came to live with Grandpa and Grandma and grew up as one of the sisters to my mama. That's why we called her Aunt Tince. Her real name is Oleta, and she was really my cousin. Grandpa included Uncle Earl's family (Earl was my mama's oldest brother) and Aunt Tince when he gave away money. Back in the mid- to late-1940s, $11,000 was a lot of money; in fact, it was something like $100,000 in today's money. A first class stamp only cost three cents back then. So Grandpa gave away about $100,000 each year from the mid-1940s to 1965 when he died. My mom got $2,000 per year (about $22,000 per year today) because Grandpa wanted to give my folks more since Mama and Daddy left their church to help Grandma when she was sick.

Grandpa had all the kids draw straws to see what property they were to inherit. Mama got the 160 acres from which we herded the cattle to go to Armour Packing Company. Mama's property had two gas wells and two oil wells, but those weren't included with the property because the mineral rights were all put together and divided equally among all the kids. Lone Star Gas Company was notified, and so was the oil company. I still don't know what happened to the money or who has it now. When oil prices were low, Aunt Ila was getting it. When prices went up . . . who knew? Maybe the State Railroad Commission had it or Aunt Ila's kids.

Aunt Ila got the eighty acres that the old homeplace sat on. She didn't want it, so Daddy and Mama bought it from her. That meant my folks owned 240 acres of the thousand or so acres total. They never cared how much it was worth and never intended to sell it or even earn a penny from owning it. They simply wanted to own part of God's great land. Technically, looking back, you could say that my parents were rich. They certainly owned a lot of land and had plenty of money in the bank. But that's not how they lived. They gave every penny they earned to the church and lived a frugal and austere life with zero luxuries. To look at them and me, and the way we lived, you'd have thought my whole family was dirt poor.

I was born in 1938 on Third Street in a brick house on a WPA brick street. The Works Progress Administration (WPA) was created in the 1930s as a part of the New Deal, FDR's gradual injection of socialism into our collective consciousness. Keep that word in mind as you analyze the use of *progress* or *progressive* in today's vernacular and political philosophy. Little by little, politicians on the left have chloroformed the public into accepting socialism (liberalism and progressivism) as a political philosophy, and in so doing, changed the free market and the Constitution. The WPA was based on doing good, but it mostly did not accomplish its objectives. The WPA told people to look forward to transcendental good times, but it ended up making people jealous of anyone who had more than they did.

FDR took over as president in 1933 during the Depression, and by 1938, when I was born, the economy was about ready to sink again. So FDR created the WPA that built all those brick streets in Cisco, all over Texas, and everywhere else. He gave us the New Deal with soup, and the American voters sold their souls for porridge like Esau in the Bible, building on the blocks of leftover socialism bequeathed by Woodrow Wilson, trying their best to create a utopia, or in other words, a socialist government expansion. To a degree, it worked like a "suckerfish" on the American public because FDR retained power from 1933 to 1945, four election cycles. Even the Democrats were concerned about America becoming a dictatorship. Today, historians consider FDR a hero, but those historians never visited Cisco, Texas. Then, and even today, you'll find many citizens in the region, especially those over the age of seventy-five, who hold less than favorable opinions of the thirty-second president of the US!

Regardless of what was happening in the outside world, those were happy days for me. Our whole Parmer family was in Cisco except Aunt Ila. She had run away with a hometown boy, J. T. Cook, who wanted to be a movie star and musician, so they moved to Hollywood and then New Jersey. New Jersey? Why would anyone want to move to New Jersey? Maybe it was because Frank Sinatra lived there.

Everybody in Cisco knew Daddy, Reverend Luther Pryor, because he had a big church, he laughed a lot, and he was married to a Parmer, Anna, my mama. One day a man came by the parsonage before I was born and asked Mama and Daddy if they could keep his youngest daughter for a few days. She was about six months old. He had previously dropped his older daughter off with his mother-in-law in Palacios, Texas, but she couldn't take both. Daddy and Mama said yes. He never came back, and his body was later found floating in the Gulf of Mexico off Galveston. And that's how Nantha Lee became my older sister. I loved her so much, and she loved me. We played together with our cousins, and we watched Mama wring chickens' necks.

Martin Luther—no, not *that* Martin Luther—Martin Luther, my older half brother, came in the back door one day after riding his bike somewhere. Mama grabbed him and spanked him while Nantha Lee and I looked on. Kids got spanked back then. It scared me to death, and I almost wet my pants. Life was too good for something like that to happen. Mama was gentle and kind. Why would she do that? Joana (Martin Luther's daughter and my niece) told me years later it was because he ripped his pants. This happened around the beginning of 1942, right before I turned four.

The church board met at the parsonage from time to time and always at night. They would talk about stuff, eat cake, and drink coffee. All us kids ran around in the front yard chasing lightning bugs. We placed the lightning bugs on our fingers, and it looked like we wore diamond rings. We ran and played and laughed. Oh, how happy we were!

Well, it was time to move . . . the Methodist tradition, the one that ol' John Wesley put in place when he came over here from England to Savannah, Georgia. He wanted all pastors to move every two years. We weren't even Methodists, although our church was kinda launched out of the Methodist tradition. Daddy pastored the Cisco church for fourteen years, and everybody loved him. They wanted him to stay until the Lord came, but since the Lord hadn't come yet, we moved. The powers that be kept up the pressure, so we finally moved to Borger, Texas. I was not quite four. The church and parsonage in Borger were right next to each other on a dirt road.

2

Borger, Texas

To the child, most new experiences are fun—at first.

Moving is a big deal, and moving to Borger was kinda fun. However, a huge question mark hung in my little mind. Living in Borger was the first time I figured out what Daddy's pastor role meant. Mama played the piano, Daddy preached, the congregation sang, *and* people said amen. Little did I know that I was sinking.

The sand blew all the time in Borger. No WPA brick streets existed where we lived, just dirt roads, except downtown where the shoe store was. Martin Luther, my brother, worked there as a shoe salesman. Kids could work back then.

One night, when the rain came down in torrents and thunder frightened me awake, I ran like crazy and jumped in bed with Mama and Daddy. When I looked up, I saw a picture of Jesus with sheep on the wall next to their bed. They always told me Jesus was a shepherd, but we didn't have any sheep. That was OK, because I knew I was safe with Mama and Daddy . . . and Jesus.

Borger is in the panhandle, the northwest part of Texas, and it snowed there. In the winter, the wind and snow blew down from Canada through Nebraska, Kansas, and Oklahoma into Texas. Mercy, it was cold. I stayed inside where it was warm, and besides, I had the mumps. We lived right next door to the church, and on Sunday morning and night, I could hear Mama playing the piano while the people sang a hymn.

> What a fellowship, what a joy divine,
> Leaning on the everlasting arms;
> What a blessedness, what a peace is mine,
> Leaning on the everlasting arms.
> (Elisha A. Hoffman, "Leaning on the Everlasting Arms," 1887)

I was about four years old, so Nantha Lee and Martin Luther were much older; consequently, they had bicycles and played with older kids. It didn't matter, because I got the mumps soon after we moved to Borger, and everyone stayed away from me. Then it got real cold, and it snowed.

Sometimes I cried because I wanted to see my mama. I got over the mumps, and sunshiny spring came. I went back to church again, and Martin Luther liked to sit with Mama on the second seat, piano side, while Daddy preached. Martin Luther always went to sleep and put his head on Mama's lap. I think he was about sixteen years old.

When spring came, that kid who owned a motorcycle burned circles round and round in the dirt between the parsonage and the church, and Mama washed clothes on the back porch. She had to be careful, though, because if the sand was blowing or the carbon black plant was puffing smoke, she couldn't hang the clothes out to dry. They'd get all dirty again.

World War II had started, and the "gubmint" (that's the way Texas people said *government*) hadn't rationed gasoline and sugar yet. The war was so bad that Martin Luther had to go, or at least he wanted to go! I think he was only about sixteen or seventeen. With a parent's approval, a kid could join the military of his choice before the age of eighteen. That way, they could avoid the draft. Since my daddy had been a doughboy in World War I, he had a real bad taste for war. But Martin Luther wanted to go, so Daddy asked him to join the Navy instead of the Army. We were terribly sad when he left for war. He was much older than me, so we weren't close, but he was my brother, and I loved him. I cried. Everybody cried. We didn't know if we'd ever see him again.

On the same day they took Martin Luther away, we got into our blue '40 model Dodge and headed for Levelland to see Arch, a longtime friend of my folks. Hallelujah! We happened to see Martin Luther again because the car taking him to war passed us heading for Amarillo. We all waved and waved. Mama cried.

My mama and daddy helped Arch as much as they could. Arch was "called" to preach through my dad's ministry in Cisco and had been a pastor of a neighboring church. Unfortunately, his wife took off and left him. Back in those days, divorce was the "unpardonable" sin in the church, so Arch had to resign. And *then* Arch committed a sin on his own—another "unpardonable" sin—he got married to another lady. Oh. My. Lard! It always confused me that we couldn't use cuss words like golly, gosh, heck, and dadgummit, but we could say *lard*. Maybe it was because when Texas country folks said *Lord*, it sounded like *lard*.

Arch could never, ever pastor a church again. Arch and his new wife had a three-year-old little girl, Arch's stepdaughter. While everyone was in the living room visiting, all of a sudden, we heard her screaming bloody murder. She was screeching, "I didn't do it! I didn't do it!"

We ran into the room, expecting to see all hell breaking loose. Arch's stepdaughter sat on the floor with the family photo album. She had taken scissors and cut most of the album into little bitty pieces, howling and squealing, "I didn't do it!"

When lying, it always helped to have someone else to blame.

I never got to know anyone in Borger 'cept Myra Lukenbill when we played in the nursery. Myra had red hair and was a child prodigy, whatever that meant. Piano. She grew up to be a concert pianist and taught music. I think she had a bunch of kids. Her folks were good friends with my mama and daddy.

Some other folks also came to church, but they couldn't join because the wife wore a gold wedding band. "Gold, or pearls, or costly array" weren't allowed—'specially lipstick. There's nothing in the Bible about lipstick. Daddy always had a hurt in his heart over those rules, but the big cheeses had their laws, and Daddy had to go along. The funny thing was I met their son again in college, and we sang together in the Collegiate Quartet from about the fall of 1956 to the end of summer 1957. An odd coincidence.

So much for Borger. We had hardly been there before it was time to move again. We left the sands of Borger and the carbon black plant behind for the Louisiana bayou. I was maybe five years old.

I didn't realize it until later, but the quick move to and from Borger was when I started my descent into sinking sand. I had no roots. How could a child know these things? Instability tossed me about like a Texas tumbleweed in the wind.

3

Lake Charles, Louisiana

Jesus loves the little children,
All the children of the world.
Red and yellow, black and white
They are precious in His sight.

— C. Herbert Woolston

The early learning experiences of children are caught more than
taught. Moving to Louisiana began a journey that sank deep in my
psyche. From this moment on, I had no place anywhere I called home.
Sinking sand began.

Lake Charles was a strange place with a unique culture, but I didn't
know it. I was happy because my folks were happy people, and they
were happy because Lake Charles was on the water. So many different
types of people lived there, you didn't know who was who—French,
white, Indian, Cajun, Negro (direct descendants of slaves), Haitian,
Creole, and Redbone.

Redbones were a mixture of everything. They had French blood,
pirate blood, Indian blood, Negro blood, and Haitian blood, and they
had a strange voodoo religion, whatever that was—all I knew, it was

17

bad. Nobody, I mean *nobody*, went into Redbone town. People thought they were the meanest of the mean.

No garbage trucks collected trash back then. A Negro man had a wagon pulled by two horses, and he came around and dumped our garbage into the back. I liked him because I liked his horses, and Mama said I could run alongside the wagon for two blocks, but then I had to come home. No African American people lived in "Louzeeanna" at that time . . . and no black people, either. Those names came along later.

Daddy always seemed to go to churches that needed help. In the beginning, the Lake Charles church was split—that's what they called it when members didn't get along with each other. Daddy preached to everyone in Lake Charles, and all the people loved him. Mama played the piano, cleaned the house, and cooked pinto beans. She also planted hydrangeas around the new parsonage Daddy bought for the church across from the old parsonage. For some reason, this helped people like each other.

The only time I had seen Daddy cry outside of the church was when we went to visit some church members who lived by the Gulf. They operated a bridge. Daddy looked to his left and saw the ship that brought him back from World War I. He pulled the car over to the side and told Mama that he came back home from France on that ship. I cried because Daddy cried.

When we arrived at the houseboat where the man and his wife lived, the husband, the bridge operator, gave me a string with bacon on it, and the crabs grabbed hold. I pulled 'em up and put them in a bucket while the grown-ups visited.

The church District Big Shot (DBS) came to visit from time to time, preached, and talked to Daddy. He always preached about women and about how they were not supposed to wear jewelry or lipstick. And, boy howdy, if they cut their hair—mercy me! It was called "bobbed" hair. So all the women wore their long hair in a bun on the back of their heads. If they had gray hair, they sure didn't dye it blue.

The DBS said things like, "The devil will put his feet in your dangling earrings, tangle his fingers in your bobbed hair, and ride your painted face to hell." I suppose he didn't like girdles either. I think he loved Isaiah 3:16–24 and 26.

> Moreover the Lord saith, Because the daughters of Zion are haughty, and walk with stretched forth necks and wanton eyes, walking and mincing as they go, and making a tinkling with their feet:
>
> Therefore the Lord will smite with a scab the crown of the head of the daughters of Zion, and the Lord will discover their secret parts.
>
> In that day the Lord will take away the bravery of their tinkling ornaments about their feet, and their cauls, and their round tires like the moon,
>
> The chains, and the bracelets, and the mufflers,
>
> The bonnets, and the ornaments of the legs, and the headbands, and the tablets, and the earrings,
>
> The rings, and nose jewels,
>
> The changeable suits of apparel, and the mantles, and the wimples, and the crisping pins,
>
> The glasses, and the fine linen, and the hoods, and the vails.
>
> And it shall come to pass, that instead of sweet smell there shall be stink; and instead of a girdle a rent; and instead of well set hair baldness; and instead of a stomacher a girding of sackcloth; and burning instead of beauty. [. . .]
>
> And [. . .] she being desolate shall sit upon the ground.

He also liked 1 Timothy 2:9. As far as the DBS knew, it meant something like women were in bad shape if they didn't adorn themselves modestly (that meant dress up properly without lipstick, of course). And if they wore braided hair with gold and pearls and a costly array, they would sure as hell go to hell. The women were also to have shamed faces and look real mad, like old Sister Horn. Yep, he really, really liked to make women feel bad. Men were OK.

On our way out to see some church people who made bread and sold it out of their home (I can still remember the wonderful smell!), Daddy stopped along the way and talked to some people who had a bunch of horses—Shetland ponies. They were all running wild and neglected. Daddy picked one out, a pinto with a mane so long it pulled his neck to the side. The next day, Daddy went back and brought him home to the parsonage. He washed him, cut his hair, and named him Tony. Tony was my first horse, and I loved him. Even though I was kicked in the stomach when I was six months old by a horse in Cisco— I had no fear of horses.

I was five years old by the time I got Tony, so I was big enough to ride on my own. Daddy went down and bought me a red one-horse wagon, perfect for Tony to pull. I rode all through the neighborhood in the wagon while Tony pulled. I made sure I didn't go into Redbone town. Back in those days, socializing with different people was frowned upon, except Daddy had some Negro singers come to church. We loved them, but the DBS wasn't pleased with that. DBSs of long ago were like union bosses—you toed the line, or you were out!

In fact, not too many sinners came to church either. I'm not sure, but I think they had to become Christians first, then they could fit in with everybody else. No lipstick, for sure, on men or women! Anyway, everyone came together before we left, and everybody lived happily ever after.

Reverend Lum Jones sat at our kitchen table after church one night. He was a traveling evangelist. His jet-black hair was greased and combed straight back, and he yelled a lot (which scared me to death). My mom made a pot of pinto beans, cornbread, and fresh onions to be eaten after church (mercy!). She had sweet milk too so we could crumble cornbread up and pour milk over it. Brother Jones ate about four bowls of beans, crunched on fresh onions, and drank sweet milk. Oh my goodness! As a little kid, I heard him groaning late, late at night.

My mom and dad ran into his room as he was groaning and said, "Brother Jones, is there anything we can do to help you?"

With his deep evangelist's voice, he said in a spiritual tone, "Do you have any more of those beans?"

It didn't end well.

Brother and Sister Murphy visited us from somewhere in Texas and a short time later moved to Lake Charles to manage the Salvation Army place. They were "called" to pastor a church when they attended Daddy's church in Cisco. When pastoring, they got crosswise with the DBS, so they joined the Salvation Army, and Brother Murphy became a captain.

No one had air conditioning, so we left windows open. They had screens over them to keep the mosquitos out, and there were lots of mosquitos in Louisiana. I was sleeping in a room by myself when a man tried to come through the window. I think he was a burglar, at least that's what I heard later. Daddy was a light sleeper, and he ran into my room and whacked the man on the head before he could climb through the window. The burglar took off like a shot. It was about 1944—before I turned six.

World War II was still raging. We couldn't go to many places because we didn't have enough stamps. See, the government issued stamps for gasoline, tires, sugar, and other things. Even if you had the money, it made no difference. You had to have rationing stamps. The war was on—it took all we had to support the effort.

Fortunately, Daddy was able to finagle some stamps, so we drove straight up north through Arkansas to see his friend Arch. By that time, Arch had moved to Cassville, Missouri, and continued to sell life insurance. Rainbow trout were plentiful there, and Daddy and Arch went fishing.

Arch's friend had a little baby with a great big head, and they thought she would die. It's called encephalitis today. Arch butchered cows in a big garage to make money. One night we went there while he was cutting meat. A big fifty-five-gallon drum was sitting in the corner with pure cow grease in it. As the curious little guy I was, I pulled myself up to look and, oops, fell in headfirst. It was a good thing Daddy and Arch happened to turn around, 'cause only my feet were stickin' out. They rushed over and pulled me out feet first.

Maybe I've been greased up ever since. In truth, it was yet another near-death experience and another stupid thing in a long list of stupid things I did in my young life. I could easily have asphyxiated if they hadn't pulled me out so fast. How I kept breathing, I don't know.

A preacher named Brother Freeman Pearson asked Daddy to come to preach somewhere in the "Louzeeanna" bayou. Brother Pearson was an insurance salesman, too. He was a pastor, and his wife wore po'folks clothes made from flour sacks. Brother Pearson told Daddy he would give him a pig if he would preach for him. Such was how Daddy was paid for preaching a "revival."

I'm not sure if anyone got revived, but I had fun playing under the house with all Brother Pearson's kids—six or eight of them. Their house was stickin' high up on stilts because, in the bayou, that's just the way it was. Everything was wet, and we had mud all over us. They were poor people and had some pigs living under their house that they would eat from time to time. They also had new twin goats, little kids. All of us laughed at them because something was wrong with them— they were both boys and girls at the same time. They called them *marfadites*. Now that I'm "edjicatid," I found out the proper name is *hermaphrodite*.

Before I could get my bearings, it was time to move again. Sinking sand. We were in Louisiana for about ten months. I only had one friend, a little boy I played with maybe one or two times. His folks weren't church folks, so we had to be careful. Daddy got a one-wheel trailer and put Tony in it and had a cage on the front of the trailer for the pig Daddy got from Brother Pearson. All day long, Daddy drove us to south Texas in our '40 model Dodge and on to Harlingen. We arrived late, late at night, and just as we pulled up in front of the parsonage, the wheel on the one-wheel trailer broke off with Tony and the pig in it. That turned out to be a bad omen. The days were like shifting sand. I turned six in August of that year.

4

Harlingen, Texas

Crises, like tests at school, are teaching moments.

In Harlingen, battles became the way of my young life. I turned six in August and started school, the first grade. I already knew all the states and every state capital. Mama gave me a chemistry set in Lake Charles, so naturally, I tried every combination of toy chemicals to blow things up. Here began a fantastic journey, experiences that changed my life forever but also left scars on my psyche that remain to this day.

Harlingen was right next to the Rio Grande River near the Gulf of Mexico. All kinds of Mexican people came over the border. Some swam across the Rio Grande to pick oranges, and local government officials rudely called them *wetbacks*, Mexicans who wouldn't go through the border gate from Matamoros. They swam across 'cause they didn't want anyone to know where they were.

Shortly after we got there, about July 1944, Pa Pryor died up in Waco. They called him Pink. He was a rough, tough guy, but somewhat small. Pa was a heavy drinker with a short temper. One day when Daddy and his brother, my Uncle Claude, were little boys—somewhere around Center or Abbott, Texas (Daddy was born in Center)—Pa got drunk, told the boys to do something, and when they didn't do it right away, he took the shotgun and said he was gonna kill 'em. They ran into the cornfield, and Pa shot toward their backs. Right before he pulled the trigger, they fell, and the tops of the cornstalks around them were shot off.

Later, Pa became a Christian, and when I was just five years old, right before I turned six in August, I sneaked into his room in Waco, and he was on his knees, praying. He died that way.

School started in Harlingen. I had never been to school because they didn't have kindergarten back in those days. Mamas were supposed to teach their kids colors and numbers and things like that before the first grade. That's why my mama bought me a chemistry set in Louisiana, a map puzzle of the United States, and spent time teaching me colors and numbers.

Our home was a happy place. The atmosphere was more important for teaching than going to kindergarten or learning about chemicals. Tony, my horse, was there, and Mama and Daddy loved each other, although people didn't show affection like they do now.

Kids made fun of me because of my funny-looking nose. I didn't know what it meant to be made fun of, and I sure didn't know what a deviated septum was. It didn't matter, and it didn't bother me too much. Tony was out back, and I saddled him up myself and rode him all the time. The resaca, a little U-shaped lake that split off from the Rio Grande, was close by, and asparagus grew all along the banks. I was thrilled to pick some and bring them to my mama.

A bunch of us kids, including the Hamm kids, went into the church one day, and I preached like my daddy. Nantha Lee, my sister, ran next door to the parsonage and told Mama, "Marshall Hall is in the church preaching." Preaching was supposed to scare the living daylights out of people and make everyone cry and go down to the mourner's bench—everyone called it the altar. So it scared Nantha Lee and the other kids, and they all knelt down crying and stuff and leaving snot on the altar. It was the first time I ever stood at an altar, and I liked how it felt. I felt confident and secure in that place, just like my daddy.

Daddy sold Tony and went across the river into Mexico and bought a Mexican saddle horse—a Lusitano used for bullfighting named Smokey. I guess Daddy thought I was growing up and needed a grown-up's horse. To me, it was a big one. A whole lot bigger than Tony, 'cause Tony was a Shetland. Daddy always made me saddle my horse and take care of him. I was so small, I had to stand on a stool Daddy made for me to saddle up. He said if I was gonna have a horse, I had to take care of it. Smokey wasn't fully broken, so Daddy made it my responsibility to "break" him. I stood on the stool, put on the bridle, saddled him, and while Daddy held him still, I climbed on wearing my stomach truss. Smokey bucked a little, not much, and off we went. We fell in love with each other. Problem was my rupture truss cut into my guts. I put up with it because that was normal, I guess. I'm not sure that at six years of age I knew what normal was and wasn't.

Daddy raised lovebirds (parakeets) in two big cages. Back in those days, people could do things and have animals that are prohibited now—sing it—"Reg-u-*lay*-shuns!"

I was so happy, but when Daddy whupped Nantha Lee because she kissed Bobby, the kid that lived behind us, it scared me to death. I also was scared when I saw an airplane with smoke coming out of the back of it. It was going round and round in the sky. I didn't know how to read yet, so I ran into the house screaming and crying to Mama, "Jesus is coming! Jesus is coming!"

Mama told me someone was writing *Pepsi Cola* in the sky.

As I matured, I questioned why the coming of Jesus would be such a bad thing. I came to understand that almost all preachers were supposed to either scare everyone about the second coming or make them feel guilty.

Even though the war was on, because Daddy was a preacher, the "gubmint" gave us a few extra stamps from time to time. We used them to go to camp meetings where there was singing and *oh my goodness*, while we were there, some preachers' wives got up and started running around in the sawdust. They called it shouting. Mama said they did it 'cause they loved Jesus. I thought I loved Jesus, too, but I never did that! I was afraid to do it because I thought people would make fun of me for having that thing in my nose.

Daddy's preaching affected me in ways I didn't understand. He didn't mean to scare people; it's what he was taught to do. Daddy told

me much later that if he had to do it over, he would do things differently. He was a "cornfield" preacher who listened to upper management (meaning other traveling preachers and big shots like Uncle
Buddy Robinson, R. T. Williams, and J. B. Chapman), and he followed
in their paths. He didn't blame them, and neither do I. Jesus understands and loves us!

Daddy didn't set out to be a preacher; the calling found him. When
Daddy got out of World War I, he became a barber in Wichita Falls,
Texas, but he didn't go to school to be a barber. Back in those days, all
you needed to do was say you wanted to cut hair, and if people liked
what you did, they would come back, and you could cut their hair
again. Daddy drank a lot of Bay Rum while he was cutting hair in
Wichita Falls. Barbers cut out tonsils way down deep in someone's
throat, and he could pull teeth, too. He gave the men Bay Rum until
they got all drunk, and Daddy reached way down in their throats and
cut the tonsils out or pulled their teeth. I guess that's why Daddy
drank Bay Rum, too. Anyway, he married his first wife, Lois Wilson,
there in Wichita Falls, Texas.

One day a friend invited Lois to go to a church called the Pilgrim
Holiness. When rough-tough men moved west, traveling preachers
put up brush arbors to have a church—in the open. Daddy and his
wife, Lois, went to the Pilgrim Holiness church and took the boys to
Sunday school. Truth be told, up to that point, Daddy probably didn't
know one church from another—he and the rest of the family weren't
churchgoers.

Daddy smoked a lot (Chesterfields) and drank more Bay Rum after
they went to church. But Daddy got to feeling bad about it 'cause his
daddy, Pink, was a big drinker and he knew it was terrible. Daddy and
his first wife went back to church and started loving Jesus. By that
time, the mid- to late-1920s, they had two boys, Howard Phillip and
Martin Luther.

After a while, Daddy started thinking he wanted to preach like
those other preachers, so he went to church one day when his wife
was sick. The people sat in a circle, and each one was supposed to
quote a verse out of the Bible. When it was his turn, he said, "I
pass."

He went home and told his wife, and she said, "Why didn't you just say, 'Jesus wept?'"

He said, "I didn't know He wept!"

Lois was sick a lot. They said it was because she had leakage of the heart. She passed away before too long from a heart attack. Daddy didn't drink Bay Rum or smoke anymore, but he had two little boys to keep. By that time, he decided he wanted to be a preacher. The Nazarenes were like the Pilgrims in many ways, but they were bigger and had a school in Hamlin, Texas. That's where he met Harold "Bro. Mac" McClain. Harold became an ordained minister later on in Cisco and served as a pastor in eighteen churches during his forty years of service to the Church of the Nazarene.

School wasn't required to be a cornfield preacher; nevertheless, Daddy went anyway. He needed his in-laws to keep the boys for a little while. His in-laws took the boys for a few months and then wouldn't give them back. Plus, they told the boys bad things about Daddy—more to Howard Phillip than Martin Luther 'cause Howard Phillip was older. This was about 1927 or 1928—give or take. Daddy had some rough edges. He got the kids back, and my mama became their mama. That all happened before I came along in 1938. By then, Howard Phillip was eighteen, and Martin Luther was about thirteen or fourteen.

Daddy went to a Nazarene academy or junior college or something in Hamlin, Texas. Mama was also going there with her double cousin Mary Cleveland. Harold introduced Daddy to Mama (Carrie Anna Parmer), and Daddy introduced Harold to Mary Cleveland. At the time, Harold wasn't a preacher; he was "called" later on in 1936. The Cisco Church of the Nazarene wanted Daddy to move there and become their pastor. When he said yes, my mama said yes to marriage and two little boys to boot. Mary was from Cisco, so Harold moved there, married Mary in 1933, and was called to preach. I guess if someone wanted to be "called to preach," they could move to Cisco.

In 1944, Harold and Mary began pastoring seven miles away from Harlingen in San Benito, Texas. Other pastors seemed to follow Daddy around. With them just seven miles away from Harlingen, we went places together with Harold and Mary and camped out along the Rio

Grande River. No motels were around back in those days. We had a tent and an ice chest with Coca-Colas, lunch meat, and fresh onions. Mama never brought pinto beans on our camping trips.

On one such camping trip with Harold and Mary, I nearly met death again in the sinking sand incident. Though Daddy and Harold rescued me, it felt so unfair and unjust. What had I done to invite disaster? The event settled in my emotions, and to me, behavior and forgiveness were inextricably tied together. Almost every day for more than seventy years, I've thought about that moment. Life is fragile and fleeting, but forgiveness does not depend on first having perfect behavior. God sent His Son into the world to "salvage" everyone!

For all practical purposes, however, my life felt normal. World War II was going on, and somehow we got stamps from the government and traveled to Colorado Springs, Colorado, with Harold and Mary to see the Broadmoor Seven Falls and Helen Hunt Jackson's grave. Indians lived there (I don't think they were Comanches). Harold and Daddy bought me a chief's headdress with feathers. I think that was the first time I heard Harold call me MAHA, which was short for Marshall Hall (gotta say it right—MarshallHall not Marshall-Hall). MAHA was a name Harold teased me about, being the first two letters of each of my names, Marshall and Hall.

Brother and Sister Murphy came up from Lake Charles and sang for our church, kind of like evangelists. They were great! She played the piano, and they sang together. Sister Murphy weighed about three hundred pounds, and the piano jumped up and down when she played. Their teenage son was an amazing organist and played the organ for a guy named Oral Roberts, but he didn't like it because he said it was just a show. Brother Murphy was called to preach when they attended the Cisco church. He was a little man from Ireland, and he sang real high notes. They weren't Nazarenes anymore.

From time to time, I rode Smokey to school and tied him to a tree. Mama or Daddy would come by later and lead him home. While I was at school, Mama and Daddy worked all around the parsonage fixin' it up. Parsonages everywhere needed fixin' up. The parsonage was always *the* parsonage, not our home. It still belonged to the church, so we never had a home of our own. Even after Daddy and Mama fixed things up real pretty inside and outside, we had to leave it all behind 'cause nothing ever belonged to us. I don't remember having any long-time friends. We never stayed long enough in one place for me to make them.

I was so proud when Mama came to school with me. She sat around with the other mamas and sewed costumes for our little drama performance. I was a woody-woodpecker. No one made fun of me for being a woody-woodpecker, but they still made fun of "that thing" sticking out of my nose. Mama and Daddy and Nantha Lee never said anything about it, so I guessed it was all right.

The kid down the street had some sores on him. I caught his sores, too. I remembered it as "infantigo"—I wasn't an infant, but I hurt anyway. Those sores got infected and ran yellow stuff all over my body. I had to stay at home. My mama painted me with some purple stuff that took it away. Only later did I learn that I had *impetigo*, a skin infection caused by bacteria.

Every day Daddy studied the Bible, worked around the church and parsonage, and took care of the birds. Mama cleaned the house and cooked pinto beans with onions. I took care of Smokey, brushed him, fed him, and cleaned his pen. I was about six years old. I learned a lesson taking care of Smokey. At first, I thought if I curried him (with a metal brush) or brushed him, his coat would be pretty and shiny. I soon learned that to make a horse's hair look all nice and beautiful, I had to make sure Smokey ate well, and soon his whole body looked great. Brushing is proper, but the food is necessary. All of us were happy.

My folks got upset when we went to visit some kinfolks because their boy took me up the street and had me smoke a cigarette. They were Camels. Not only was I a six-year-old and small for my age, but the boy physically, emotionally, and verbally bullied me.

I didn't understand it then, but that malignity—along with bullying about my size and the "thing" sticking out of my nose—traumatized my soul, and the combined toxicity forever savaged my heart. I never had awful feelings before that, but I did from that day on for the next decade of my life. The events of that day dramatically changed both my frame of mind and my personality. I felt shame and embarrassment and never mentioned the details of what happened to anyone, least of all my parents, until I wrote these words.

I wish I had spoken up sooner. To anyone who is forced to suffer indignities at the hands of sociopaths or poisonous people, I can tell you with certainty that God wants you to unburden your soul. We can't change the past, but we can learn from it and use it to make our lives better.

In my case, a volcano of grief and anger boiled deep down where only I lived. I guess it may have caused revenge and guilt even though I didn't know what it meant. Up until then, I had always been happy because Mama and Daddy were happy. I guess little kids can't intellectualize their feelings. Maybe that's why for children, things are felt more than telt.

Most people will live their entire lives never knowing who they are. Only the glorious power of a cleansing and loving friendship with the great God of heaven inspired me to *never give up!* In those early years, however, before I knew God, most of my energy went to fuel the wellspring of anger inside me.

Children can know God, but in my case, I think knowing God was more of a cultural thing than a personal experience. Even Jesus told people to bring the kids to Him. In Matthew 19:14 NIV, He said, "Let the little children come to me, and do not hinder them, for the kingdom of heaven belongs to such as these."

My traumatic near-death and abusive experiences in Harlingen, Texas, hurt me deeply. Nevertheless, I guess I loved Jesus, because I went to church all the time.

Time to move.

No friends.

Sinking sand.

5

Back to Cisco

Back in the saddle again. The place of my birth. Breathing the fresh air of ranch life.

Cisco was always a sort of home, but before this, we were seldom there except to visit. All of my cousins were there, and I could ride my horse all over Grandpa's ranch. I never had to worry about kids teasing me, because out on the ranch, I had only chickens, pigs, cattle, horses, and a thousand other kinds of animals for company. And I was growing up. Riding the school bus into Cisco made me feel like a grown-up.

Grandma Parmer, out on the ranch in Cisco, got real sick. She had skin cancer all over her body, and the ones on her nose and arms were really bad. They said it was because she worked out in the sun. Plus, she had old-agers disease (probably Alzheimer's before anyone realized what it was). I had barely completed the second grade in Harlingen before we moved again. Mama had to take care of Grandma, and Daddy had to travel around to preach. Daddy told the people at the church in Harlingen we were moving back to Cisco. They all cried, and I did too. It felt just like floundering in quicksand. So confusing.

Because Daddy had to go into the evangelistic field (I didn't know what that meant), he was able to get some stamps for gasoline, but he couldn't get any for tires. The trailer was packed with our stuff and Smokey too. We had already eaten the pig. The trunk was full, and the inside of the car was packed, and everything else was on top of the car. Daddy hitched a trailer to our '40 model Dodge, and we took off. We still had the old Dodge because almost no cars were built in the United States from about 1941 to 1945. The first cars after the war were in 1946. Daddy, Mama, Nantha Lee, Mickey (our Pekingese dog), Smokey, and I all took off for Cisco. We left the lovebirds (parakeets) with some church folks. We moved back just before I turned eight.

On the road back, two tires blew out on the car at the same time. We didn't have any stamps to buy tires because rubber was in short supply, so we sat along the road for two days—waiting! No motels existed back then, no AAA, and no one to call (cell phones didn't come along for another forty years). Eventually, Daddy walked somewhere into a town, and the Nazarene pastor there got us a few stamps to get tires. Daddy rolled both tires down the side of the road for I don't know how many miles. He carried the tubes around his neck. I don't remember how he pumped the tires up. I just remember he worked hard at it while I walked Smokey around. What an inauspicious return.

Insecurity and anger stewed in my heart, but I didn't realize it. That genesis of insecurity, however, became a strong foundation and the source of my determination to overcome every obstacle I faced. With no friends and my parents both immersed in church business, I was left to my own devices most of the time.

Grandpa lived way out north of Cisco on a ranch. He had about a thousand cows (and some bulls, too), and he had a name for each one, or it seemed that way. Those animals became my friends, the only ones I had (except my cousins, who lived about two or three miles away on a dirt road). I walked through the herd, and they let me pet them. They didn't hurt me, and they didn't say anything about my nose or my small size. Grandpa let me give them cow-cake, and they loved it.

Early in the morning, Mama put wood in and lit the great big ol' kitchen stove so all of us could have breakfast. Grandpa always got up first and started another fire in the meetin' room where he and Grandma slept and went around lighting the coal-oil (kerosene) lamps so we could see. The meetin' room was where everybody gathered. It had a radio in it and a crank telephone. Mama had to be careful when she talked on the phone because Mable (the operator) would listen in. I guess the meetin' room was similar to our modern-day dens except for the bed. In the winter, it became a gathering place because the fire was there. Of course, everyone spent time in the kitchen, too. When Mama cooked breakfast, the smell of homemade biscuits (she put butter and sorghum syrup on them), thick pieces of bacon right out of the smokehouse, streaked gravy, and fresh eggs got us all in a good mood. It took Grandpa about an hour to eat 'cause he didn't have any real teeth, just false ones. Even so, those were happy times.

Living in the country was so much fun because I'd see whooping cranes, bobcats, snakes of all kinds, armadillos, a few wolves, and buzzards almost as big as vultures. If I had known better, I would have been scared or at least more careful, but I left wild animals alone, and they left me alone.

The Parmer family kids lived in the country with us—Jackie Earl, Coy, Van, Billy Rex, and my sister, Nantha Lee.

When I wanted to go see Jackie Earl, Mama said, "Marshall Hall, you be careful now."

So I took off catty-corner through the pasture and walked about a mile or so to Jackie Earl's house. Sometimes I was scared when I saw a bobcat or a deer, but I just screamed, and they ran away. I made sure I didn't step on any devil's cushions, because they could hurt real bad. *Devil's cushion* was a country name for a kind of cactus, because if you stepped on it, it hurt like hell—but we couldn't say *hell* 'cause that was a bad word and church folks had to say only good words. Didn't matter—it still hurt like hell. My cousins could say *hell* because their folks didn't care.

Nantha Lee and I wanted a house pet because, for some reason, Mickey the Pekingese was gone. Maybe he died. We went down to the pigpen and got a little piggy from the litter. It was the runt, white and pink. We washed it and *tried* to make it our house pet. It didn't work! A pig is a pig is a pig is a pig. Mama made us take it back after about one day.

Refrigeration, running water, indoor toilet? No way. The water on

Grandpa's ranch was salty, and we had a two-holer about fifty feet behind the cellar. The cellar was where all the food was stored. Mama and Aunt Lillian had canned green beans and beets, cabbage, carrots, other vegetables, and all kinds of the good stuff in mason jars. Daddy had his Army things he brought home from World War I down there, too. Once in a while, a snake would get in there. Most of the time, it was a bull snake, but once in a while, we found a rattlesnake. We had to be careful.

At night we all had a slop jar in the house for us to go pee. It was too scary to go to the outhouse. Foxes, wolves (maybe only one), bobcats, and boogers might get us! We didn't have electricity either. The "gubmint" REA (Rural Electrification Act) hadn't come our way yet. Later on, Daddy bought an engine that made electricity and built Mama a washhouse out back. He ran some wires in the house, and we took down the coal-oil lamps—some upper-class people called them kerosene lamps. If we wanted to see, we had to go outside to the washhouse and start up the engine. Sometimes the engine wouldn't start, so we kept a few lamps inside just in case.

When it was getting cold, Grandpa and Daddy (if he was home) killed a calf or hog. The meat was kept in the smokehouse on benches where Daddy and Grandpa rubbed the meat with salt or brown sugar. We didn't have a refrigerator. We always killed chickens right before we ate them. Nothing compares to the smell of home-cooked country food. Nantha Lee and I chased the chickens and ran like crazy out to the cow lot, climbing the ladder up into the barn loft to see if we dared to jump down below into the hay. It was hot up there. Sometimes Grandpa made us shuck corn; mercy, that hurt our hands, but it was fun work.

We were thrilled when Mama called us to come in for supper. Years later, I heard ol' Jimmie Davis sing his song "Suppertime." I cried at the lyric, "We're going home at last."

The only thing was, Mama threw the leftovers in a five-gallon bucket along with sour milk, and I had to carry the bucket out to the pigpen every night. That was my chore. I didn't mind taking the bucket down there, even though it was heavy, and I spilled some of it on my legs. The pigs snorted and grunted as they tried to eat my toes through the slats when I poured the bucket of slop over the fence.

Our cistern was right outside the back door, and it had the coldest water I ever drank. We brought some of it into the kitchen in a wood bucket, and everyone drank out of the same dipper. We didn't have water like they had in town.

That summer of 1946, right before I turned eight, Daddy took us to the Abilene district camp meeting outside Cisco where the lake was. Cisco had the world's biggest outdoor zoo at that time; at least that's what they said. People from Texas liked to brag. We ate hamburgers from the hamburger stand with a great big ol' slice of onion and drank Hi Ho orange "sody" pop, and grape, too. As a little guy, I sat on the front seat in the sawdust listening to the pastors' wives play evangelistic piano music. There's a difference between evangelistic playing and pounding the piano. Believe it or not, I can hear it now as the people sang:

> Down at the cross where my Savior died,
> Down where for cleansing from sin I cried,
> There to my heart was the blood applied;
> Singin', glory to His name!
> Oh, precious fountain that saves from sin,
> I am so glad I have entered in;
> There Jesus saves me and keeps me clean;
> Singin', glory to His name!
> (Elisha A. Hoffman, "Down at the Cross," 1878)

I didn't remember the words, but I remembered the music all these years later. I wouldn't be surprised if some would say, "He's just an old man trying to remember this stuff." T'ain't so! Music from that day stayed with me, deep in my heart, even as the sands shifted in my soul.

In that same camp meeting, I heard J. B. Chapman preach. He was a general superintendent, the highest elected office of the Church of the Nazarene. I can't tell you what he said, but he was there preaching, and I heard him.

Church was always a big part of our life in Cisco because Grandpa and the other Parmers were some of the first Methodist Episcopal Church South people to arrive in Eastland County back in the mid- to late-1800s. Then the Nazarenes came along, so they all joined them. Later on, Daddy became the pastor there. It didn't matter if it was rain or snow; we went to church even on Wednesday night for prayer meetings. One of my funniest memories was when Grandpa stood up to testify and lost his false teeth outta his mouth, and they slid under the pews all the way up to the altar on the tile floor. Maybe those teeth wanted to be saved! Nantha Lee and I laughed and laughed until Mama threatened to spank us if we didn't stop making fun of Grandpa.

I was going into the third grade, and I was eight. Here's a picture of me—the Cisco kid, only the real one, before the 1950 television series!

Mama had to enroll Nantha Lee and me in school, and from then on, we rode the bus. Cecil McClellan drove the bus, and all the kids hated him, especially the Cozzart and Cleveland boys. Country kids are a rowdy lot, and Cecil didn't like fighting on the bus, so he would stop and kick kids off. It didn't matter where it was or how dangerous it was or how old the kids were. Parents didn't mind 'cause they said the kids deserved it.

The night before school, we always had to take a bath in the big ol' tin tub. Mama poured warm water in it that she boiled on the woodstove. Our bath was always in the kitchen. Nantha Lee didn't want anyone in there when she took a bath 'cause she was a girl. We had to get up real early. I think about five in the morning. After breakfast, we ran as fast as we could to the bus so we wouldn't be late. If we were late, even a minute, Cecil would take off and leave us behind. The bus came down the dirt road about a hundred yards from the house.

In the first week of school, I fell in love with a pretty little girl. I guess it was love, but who knows. I liked her. We talked and laughed and played on the monkey bars. She had blonde hair, and sometimes we would play marbles with the other kids. No one ever said anything about my nose, and we laughed a lot. It seemed I was getting my innocence back. The anger ebbed.

Daddy had an Underwood typewriter. I knew my ABCs. Mama taught them to me when we lived in Lake Charles, and besides, I was in the third grade like a grown-up. Nantha Lee had some sheet music songs, and I found one with a blue picture on it. I spent hours and hours late into the night typing on my daddy's Underwood preacher typewriter on the floor, copying letter by letter words to the song, "Peg O' My Heart." Nantha Lee helped me. She could read, so she told me what to do.

The day before Nantha Lee and I were to catch the bus to school, I followed my cousins into the hills behind our ranch house. They said we were going to chase raccoons, but they wanted to sneak off and smoke cedar bark wrapped in Sears and Roebuck catalog paper. The catalog was supposed to be used in the two-holer (or maybe corncobs), but they rolled up cedar bark and blew smoke. They were like the Katzenjammer Kids in the comic strip. Coy and Jackie Earl even lit a cherry bomb when Aunt Leona was sitting in the two-holer. When it went off, she ran out with her dress up, screaming like crazy! They got in trouble for doing that.

Well, back where the cow tank was, and not far from one of the oil wells, a skunk ran under one of those big sand rocks that Cisco is noted for—a perfect target for my older cousins. One of them broke a small, forked limb from a mesquite tree and said, "Marshall Hall, take this stick over there and look under the rock. We'll get on top of the rock and jump up and down while you twist the skunk's tail and pull 'im out."

Uh-oh!

The spray hit me right in the eyes! Howling and screaming and crying, I pleaded with the Lord, "Please, Jesus, don't let me go blind! Oh, save me, Jesus!" All that while, my cousins laughed their asses off.

And guess what? That little girl who I thought was destined to be my love for life would not accept my illustrious typing of "Peg O' My Heart" because she said I smelled like a skunk. That's why I still wear sweet-smellum to this day.

I don't regret those experiences. Disappointment can cut deeply, but it can also be the impetus toward strengthening the soul. Some people, perhaps most, live their whole life never knowing who they are because they have never been tested or faced "skunks" and cousins in their life. Those same cousins made sure I knew how to swim. They made a little raft out of mesquite limbs, and the three of us floated out on the cow tank (like a small lake) that was as deep as a windmill is tall. While out in the middle, they pushed me off so I would learn to swim. They went back to shore and watched me "swim" while they laughed. Vulnerable little guys must always fight harder.

When Christmas came around, Jackie Earl dressed up as Santa Claus and all the Parmer relatives came to Grandpa's house for Christmas Eve. Everyone was happy, and so was I, because Daddy and the Parmers were happy people—except Grandma, 'cause she was sick.

My big brother, Martin Luther, came home from the war when he didn't get killed. He was amazing, and so good at doing a lot of different things! He took a big block of wood and made me a truck for my Christmas present, plus he gave me a shiny metal pin to put on my bicycle when I got one, a shield that was blue on top and an American flag on the bottom. Then he went to embalming school in Dallas. Martin Luther probably saw terrible things in Guam and other places during World War II when he served in the US Navy, and he was always a guy who wanted to help people. Maybe that's why he went to embalming school. He liked to dress up and make people feel comfortable, too. He was my hero, bigger than life, and also a true American, a decorated hero in the war.

My brother, Martin Luther, in Guam, circa 1942.

Later on, Jackie Earl rode his bicycle to Grandpa's and tried to teach me how to ride. It was a big one with a bar from the seat to the handlebar section—a boy's bike. Even at eight or nine years old, I was small for my age. It didn't matter; I consider everything a challenge. My feet slipped off the pedals all the time, and that's the way I learned to ride a bike. It was also the way I almost became a eunuch.

Daddy was gone a lot as a traveling preacher, but some of the time, he was home. When he was, we went to church together at the Cisco Nazarene Church. Sister Horn was my Sunday school teacher. I had to behave. Sister Horn told my daddy that I crawled over a "banch" on Sunday morning. She told him of my crime after the service one Sunday night when some of the women fell on the floor in front of the altar, praying. Some of them looked like they were asleep, but Mama said they were under the Spirit. Daddy said he didn't know if they really were. Maybe they just needed a nap.

Old Sister Horn told Daddy I deserved a whupping 'cause I had climbed over a bench. She said, "You gotta whup that boy, or he's a-gonna grow up bad!"

And so he did. I got whupped on the way home when Daddy

pulled the car over, took his belt off, and whipped me in front of the headlights. I never liked Sister Horn after that. I think she was the only woman the city of Cisco condemned for wearing her girdle. They only gave her two weeks to get out. She made me so mad at the time, I would have put her picture on the cover of the *Watchtower* magazine.

Sister Horn was a relative of Roy Rains. The Rains had a whole bunch o' kids, and they all had names that sounded alike. Waddell was the oldest, and then came the rest. I "kain't" remember them all, but they sounded like Ardell, Udell, Arnell, and one or two more boys. Then came along Roselle, Moselle, and Myrtle Lee. They named Myrtle Lee differently because they said they had to quit having more kids. Wherever Daddy and Mama moved, they followed us. When we went to Borger later on, the Rains moved there, too.

One time, Daddy had gone preaching. Burning in my memory is the sobbing and crying of my mother as we rushed down the road in Grandpa's old black '40 model Dodge to the Callaways—distant relatives or relatives by marriage, I don't know.

In the mid-1940s, people fended for themselves. This group of Callaways was as po' as Job's turkey, and it had to lean up against the fence to gobble. They lived up the road past the Clevelands, farther out in the country than Grandpa did. In my little eight-year-old mind, I just didn't understand; I had never seen a house fire before. As we pulled into the open gate off the dirt road, the house was shooting flames that musta been a hunnerd feet high.

The Callaways were sitting on the ground with their two little kids, crying their eyes out. Even at my age, I couldn't understand why God didn't put a stop to the fire like everybody asked Him to. The house burned to the ground. They were left worse than poor—homeless with ashes all around and all their "chikins" scattered hither and yon. A couple of pigs were rootin' around. They had lived under the house, so their house was gone, too. All the grown-ups just sat on the ground with the Callaways, staring at the smoke and ashes. None of the grown-ups even thought about praying at that moment. All the folks in that part of the country helped the Callaways with food and stuff until they could get back on their feet again. Everyone had food because they either grew it or raised it.

In the summertime, we had to round up the cattle, put them on big cattle trucks, and send them to Armour Packing Company in Fort Worth. Grandpa made a lot of money doing this. Uncle Ira and Uncle Marshall, Daddy and Grandpa, and one or two Clevelands all met down on the 160-acre pasture to round up cattle as the trucks came in. That was where one of Grandpa's Lone Star gas wells was. I was still at home.

Jackie Earl and Coy never did stuff like that with us. I guess they were too busy smokin' cedar bark. I rode Smokey about three miles to the corral, and then we all spread out, rounding up the cows.

Those great big ol' cattle trucks were waiting when Smokey and I made it.

Grandpa yelled, "Marshall Hall, where you been? We got work to do."

Grandpa didn't realize that as I was riding from the homeplace, Smokey got scared and bolted, and I couldn't stop him. He ran under a mesquite tree, and a branch hit me right in the face and neck and well-nigh killed me, almost knocked me off. Good thing I was a little guy and a kid. Anyone bigger could have been killed. The pain was intense, and I thought I was gonna die. All I know is that my neck and face hurt so bad. I was scared, too, but no one gave me a second thought or any sympathy. There was work to do.

Grandpa's cows were the only ones Armour would accept if they had cancer-eyes, because Grandpa had a formula for curing cancer-eyed cows. It didn't work on Grandma. He unfortunately took the formula with him to the grave.

Grandpa let us rest once in a while beside the cow tank. It was so pure and clean, except where the cows went poo. All of us just lay down and drank water right out of the pond. We had fixings that Mama made for us for dinner (when people ate lunch, it was called dinner—breakfast, dinner, and supper).

One day, Grandpa was plowing the field between the barn and the oil well with the great big ol' workhorses. They were kind of like the Clydesdale horses in Budweiser advertisements. To him they weren't special, they were just workhorses, but they were as big as Clydesdales. Grandpa didn't drink beer, and neither did the Nazarenes. I think the Methodists did. I went out to watch Grandpa and see if he'd let me drive the horses. He could plow a row as straight as an arrow.

I can do that, I thought.

I jumped on the plow as the horses were pulling it.

"Grandpa, can I drive the horses?"

"You sure can," he said.

The rows had to be straight, 'cause the rain had to go into the ground just right, and besides, when Grandpa harvested the high gear, straight rows were ideal. As I was driving the horses, I looked back, and the row was crooked like a snake. I pulled back on the reins and stopped the horses.

"Grandpa, the rows are crooked. What am I s'pose to do?"

Grandpa said, "You just learned a good lesson, boy. You gotta keep your eye on the fence post up ahead."

Grandpa didn't act mean to me. He just taught me a good lesson for life. "Keep your eye on the fence post!"

And you know what? I looked between the two horses as I used the reins to guide them, kept my eyes on the fence post, and sure 'nuff, the rows were straight as an arrow.

"Keep your eyes on the fence post!"

Or, as Kittie L. Suffield wrote in "God is Still on the Throne" in 1929, "Keep your eyes on the prize, for the home in the skies; God is still on the throne."

Across the road from the old homeplace in the hills stood some big, flat sand rocks that the Parmers carved their names on since the mid-1800s. Great Grandpa, Great Grandma, and all the aunts, uncles, cousins—everyone. A few years ago, big landowners came through and bought the property. I don't know why, but they uprooted all the mesquite trees with big bulldozers and tore up all the rocks with a hundred years of history on them. Cacti are all that's there now.

Great big ol' buzzards live in that part of the country—or used to. Sometimes they would get hungry and try to eat little animals that were still alive. They especially liked small animals that didn't run fast enough, because they just wanted to sit and eat. I don't know why, but a whole bunch of 'em were standing around talking to each other about fifty yards off the road when I was walking to Jackie Earl's house. They were as big as vultures. Later on, in school, I learned they might have been buzzards. I don't know if they were or not, but they were as tall as I was. They looked over at me and strode my way. I skedaddled outta there in a hurry! Just think, they could have eaten me.

My grandma's sister came to visit us one time. I guess that would make her my great-aunt, wouldn't it? Anyway, she scared Nantha Lee and me to death because she was a rough, tough old Texas woman, plus she brought a spittoon. She dipped snuff as it drained down the sides of her mouth, and then she would spit into that spittoon. It left brown stuff all across the room. Mama was glad when she left, because Mama liked things to be clean. These are fond memories for me, even though at the time they didn't seem like good ol' days, especially when I slopped the hogs.

Harold and Mary McClain moved up north from San Benito to Gainesville so they could be closer to Cisco where my folks lived. Harold was called to be the pastor at the Nazarene Church in Gainesville. Mary was a Cleveland and was born and raised about five miles from the Parmers out north of Cisco. I don't know how those things work, but Mama and Mary were double cousins. I think Mary came from Uncle Will or Uncle Henry's side of the Parmer family.

After a short time, Harold and Mary left when Harold was called to a big church in Dover, New Jersey. They couldn't pass it up. I still haven't figured out how the Lord can "call" someone to a specific church. It helps to decide sometimes if the new church pays more money, but not so much for my family. Grandma died, so Daddy and Mama decided the right thing to do was to take over the church in Gainesville where Harold had been pastor. Yep. Time to move again. It seemed we always moved in the summer so Nantha Lee and I didn't have to miss school.

At nine years of age, going on ten, I was physically a lot smaller than everyone else my age and probably less mature in other ways too. Leaving Cisco was upsetting and disorienting. Why did we have to move again? It sure felt like sinking sand.

6

Gainesville, Texas

Multiple moves can take their toll on children. Counterintuitively, the pathology of anxiety can, however, bring a sense of wholeness. Strange as it may seem, a place of quiet rest exists near God when He speaks in a spiritual language.

Maturity may relate to age or the way society determines how a person is supposed to act at a certain age. That said, ten- or eleven-year-olds aren't known for clear and logical thinking. Moving eight times (Cisco, Borger, Lake Charles—twice, Harlingen, Cisco—again, and now Gainesville) took its toll. I matured fast in Gainesville and concluded that I needed a job to earn my own living.

When we moved to Gainesville, Smokey lived on a vacant lot behind the parsonage, and I took care of him even when he had big ol' ticks on his body. Those ticks sucked blood and swelled up, turning purple. Smokey's undercarriage thingy grew so big that we had to get medicine from Grandpa, so everything turned out OK.

Wednesday nights were always horrible. We had to go to a prayer meeting at the church, which was next door to the parsonage. I thought I loved Jesus, but I wasn't sure. I knew one thing for sure—I didn't like prayer meetings! When people stood up and testified, it was just awful. Old Brother Chillywaters—no, that wasn't his real name, it's just a name we gave him—he always stood up at testimony time, saying with a shaky voice, "When I cross those chilly waters of Jordan—" Blah, blah, blah.

Then everybody would get down on their knees to pray, and it hurt so much. I thought I would die. We had to stay there sometimes for what felt like a hunnerd hours. An outhouse stood behind the church—it was a one-holer for all the church to use—so sometimes I acted like I had to go pee. It got me out of staying on my knees for so long.

Daddy traded in the '40 model Dodge and bought a new car since this was after the war, and they built cars again. Everyone was wide-eyed looking at those new cars. The cars of 1946 through 1950 were amazing—DeSotos, Lincolns, Packards, Fords, Chevys, Hudsons, Nashes, Chryslers, Oldsmobiles, Cadillacs, Studebakers, Mercurys, Frazers, Kaisers, and even Plymouths. The cars looked like airplanes. If I see pictures of them, I'll jump for joy even today like everyone did back in those days.

Well, Daddy bought a Kaiser. It was the cheaper of the twins, Kaiser and Frazer. Mr. Kaiser built ships for the war and started a hospital company to take care of his workers. I think he was rich. The good part about those cars was that most of the pieces were inter-changeable (I didn't know that word back then). The Frazers were more expensive than the Kaisers.

Lloyd Davis was Nantha Lee's boyfriend. He had come home from the war in his white Navy suit and won Nantha Lee's heart, but she was only sixteen years old by that time. To keep me from seeing them, Lloyd always—always—gave me at least a quarter, and sometimes a whole dollar, so I could run down to the new Dairy Queen and buy an ice cream cone. Do you know how much a dollar would be today? About $10.00! *Wow!* His bribery gave them time to kiss and stuff.

The drugstore in Gainesville was across from the courthouse square, and they sold Coca-Colas and ice cream and lots of other stuff, but it was just too far for me to go all the way downtown on the square from Richey Street. It must have been at least ten blocks. It wasn't dangerous to go there because people drove slow, maybe twenty-five miles an hour. Gainesville had a lot of older people. I went to the Dairy

Queen because it was a lot closer—only about three or four blocks away.

Martin Luther met Joy Whisenant, a church girl. Her mom had all girls, and they all went to church. She was about eighteen years old. Joy was the oldest, or maybe the next to the oldest, of the Whisenant girls, and they were all pretty. Martin Luther liked pretty girls, so they got married. Martin Luther took her to Dallas where the embalming school was, but from time to time, they came home to visit us in Gainesville.

Late one night while Joy was having their first child—his name was gonna be Edward Luther—Nantha Lee's boyfriend Lloyd was taking coffee to the hospital on Richey Street in Daddy's Kaiser. The coffee pot was sitting on the seat next to him, and the front seat was like a sofa. Hospitals didn't have cafeterias in those days. The pot tipped over in the seat, and he grabbed it, slightly turning to the right, and slammed into the back of another car or a tree or something. It tore the whole front end of the Kaiser away. No problem, except Lloyd got all cut up. Daddy went to a junkyard and bought a wrecked Frazer for parts. Night after night, Daddy put it all together—and suddenly, we had a Kaiser that looked like a Frazer.

Next door to the parsonage was a little house where a lady named Mary lived with her real old mother. Mary was disabled. She had no legs, and her arms were twisted. She opened a little store in her house—it looked just like a 7-Eleven store. Gainesville didn't have 7-Elevens in 1948. Disability welfare didn't exist, and Mary had no other source of income, so she started her own little business. All us kids went in there and bought ice cream and candy and lots of other stuff. The grown-ups also bought things from her.

Sometimes she got cranky 'cause some of the kids would steal candy from her, and since she didn't have any legs, she couldn't chase 'em. I didn't blame her, and I didn't take anything. Jesus would get me, and my Daddy would whup the life outta me with his razor strop. Daddy and Mama were nice to her and her mama, too, even though her mama was really grouchy.

Mary didn't like the Nazarenes, but that was OK. Daddy was a happy guy, and Mama was sweet to her. Even though the bread and stuff were more expensive at Mary's, they bought stuff 'cause they felt sorry for her. Wouldn't you know it, before long, Mary changed her attitude toward Jesus and the Nazarenes. I think she started loving Jesus—anyway, she changed her mind and even came to church once in a while. I pushed her in her wheelchair since she didn't have legs, and her arms couldn't do much of anything either. It was fun doing that.

Little did Mary know, she was sitting on a veritable gold mine. My friend and a pretty close relative, Lula Belle (she was a Whisenant girl), told me that Mary and her mother had some property out west of town, and when Mary died, she willed the mineral rights to that property to the Nazarene Church. Sure enough, they struck oil there—millions of dollars worth—and the Nazarenes still get a check every month, and will for as long as there is oil in the ground. Maybe the Nazarenes should name their church building after my mama and daddy for being so kind to Mary.

That's how it goes in the ministry. It's always better to be kind to people and love them through Jesus, whether you get anything for it or not, 'cause you never know how the Lord will use it.

> Be not forgetful to entertain strangers: for thereby some have
> entertained angels unawares.
> (Hebrews 13:2 KJV)

Still, do you know what makes my heart ache? To this day, the Gainesville Nazarene Church only has about ten people who attend!

When we lived in Gainesville, the members of the church had all kinds of businesses, so one day I asked a guy who had a hay farm, Mr. Roach, if I could work for him. Although I was only eleven years old, I could drive because Nantha Lee and I would drive Grandpa's old car around the dirt roads on the ranch. Anyway, I talked Mr. Roach into letting me drive his orange Allis-Chalmers tractor and pull his hay baler. His name was "Skinny" Roach. I guess he was skinny. I don't know why or where he got the name Roach.

The Sissons were there too, and they had a boy who was crippled, but he could drive their Pontiac. The Adairs had a son who was curious—a little guy. He went with his daddy to work at the flour mill, and one day he was looking over the side of the elevator when it was going up to the next floor. It crushed his head. It was awful—just awful!

Daddy made the national news on July 17, 1949. The night when Nantha Lee and Lloyd were getting married, Daddy was on the back porch cleaning his pants with something called naphtha. There weren't dry cleaning stores in Gainesville, so Daddy cleaned his Sunday go-to-meeting clothes with naphtha. It was kind of like gasoline; at least it smelled like it. Maybe that's why he always smelled like gasoline when he preached. Well, anyway, Daddy had a pan full of naphtha, and he put his pants in there and shwooooosh—the fumes caught fire from the gas water heater on the back porch and started a house fire. The headlines all over the world read: "Preacher Burns Pants at Wedding."

An article entitled, "Pastor's Pants Catch Fire," from the *San Bernardino Sun* wrote that Daddy was badly burned, but "came back to the parsonage and performed the wedding for his daughter, Nantha Lee Pryor, and Lloyd Davis of Gainesville" after he went to the hospital.

Daddy received some letters from different places. Most were funny. The back of the parsonage burned, but Daddy rebuilt it. No one laughed about the incident in our house.

I guess I was a talker back then. People used to say I would "argy" (argue) with a signpost. The Shasteen boys lived out on a cotton farm, and I convinced them to let me help pick cotton. Talk about work . . . whooee! Those Shasteen boys grew up and made something of themselves. One of them married another Whisenant girl—Freddie, I think. Marrying a Whisenant girl meant you were top-of-the-line! That Shasteen boy went on to get a medical doctor's degree even though he picked cotton when he was a little boy.

Lula Belle Whisenant didn't marry a Shasteen. Lula Belle was my girlfriend sometimes—on-again, off-again. I really didn't know what it was all about, but we had fun. Her mother's food smelled so good, though. Defining happiness was hard, but I felt happy. I had a friend, a job, and a supportive family. Sometimes I long for those days. Lula

Belle stayed in Gainesville, lived a joyful life, married a good man, had a beautiful family, and became a schoolteacher. Later on, she would sit on her front porch in the swing, happy as a lark.

One day, my daddy came home and out of a clear blue sky told us we were moving—just like that!

Sinking sand.

The rug got pulled out from underneath me, and we had to move to Carlsbad, New Mexico. We couldn't take Smokey, so Daddy sold him. In a heartbeat, I lost everything.

Gainesville made an indelible impression on our whole family, because both Martin Luther and Nantha Lee married kids from there. Would you believe I don't have even one memory of our move to Carlsbad? I think maybe the sand was sinking a little more, perhaps a lot.

7

Carlsbad, New Mexico

If one thing doesn't work, fix it or try something else.

All of a sudden, it seemed like the crush of life pushed me into a pit from which I couldn't extricate myself. Moving and moving again, no horse, growing up, no friends. I realized how important it was to have stability and companionship.

Despite my constant exposure to church life, I had no understandable relationship with the Almighty—*understandable* being the key word.

Maturity came slow. Much of it didn't matter because I learned to adapt. A man who would later become a friend of mine, professor, writer, and minister, W. T. Purkiser, wrote *When You Get to the End of Yourself*, a book he published in 1970. In it, he said, "Trouble allowed to fester within the heart turns to tragedy. Trouble overcome by the vigor of a healthy spiritual life turns to triumph." It seemed I was betwixt and between maturity and spiritual hunger.

When we moved to Carlsbad, the potash Union of Mine, Mill, and Smelter Workers was in the midst of a seventy-three-day labor strike in 1949. I was only eleven years old, but I knew right away we were coming into a volatile and hostile new environment. I was glad to leave Gainesville, but living in Carlsbad required adjustments for which I was not prepared.

Potash is a natural mineral found in desolate places and used in fertilizer. It's dug out of the earth through deep shafts similar to ones used in coal mining. The work is hard, dirty, dangerous, and generally higher paying, but in some places like Carlsbad, it was the only meaningful work that men could find.

The union people were against everyone, especially the "scabs." The way I remember it, the "scabs" were sweet-spirited people wanting to make a living supporting their families. The biggest of all the big shots in town was the president of the International Union of Mine, Mill, and Smelter Workers, and he was also the biggest big shot in our church. Not coincidentally, he was also chairman of the church board and Sunday school superintendent. The union members of our church stood on the line going into the mines with baseball bats, hitting the buses of some of our church members who were not union members. I don't think they were sanctified. As they say in Texas, "Hep us 'n' bless us." It was awful, just awful.

Daddy was a happy man and a good preacher in Carlsbad, and Mama played the piano and cooked pinto beans like usual. We always had fresh onions, too. I played the church organ. Pretty soon, everybody came together through love, and thank God, the strike ended. Hard feelings stewed a little bit, but Daddy stayed there for eight years, and he helped people get over it.

During the seven years I was there before I went to college, more and more, I felt the sand sinking around me. Maybe it was because I was horribly bullied, at least until I learned to fight back. No longer innocent, I was taken over by a fit of deep-seated anger.

We moved so often, I found it hard to make any long-lasting friends. No, I'm not complaining—it was just a fact. I think never having friends contributed to some of my anger. The tension with the people in the church also directly affected me, because I had no life apart from the church. One thing after another generated frustration and anger.

Shortly after we arrived in Carlsbad, Mama and Daddy were out visiting folks when a knock came on the parsonage door. I ran to answer it, and two men in suits asked if Daddy was there. About that time, Mama and Daddy drove up in the '49 Plymouth Daddy bought right after we moved to Carlsbad. I told the men, "Here's my Daddy now." They came in the front door of the parsonage as Daddy entered from the back door to meet them. Then they asked if my mama and I could leave the room so they could talk to Daddy alone.

At the time, I thought the parsonage was big, but in truth, it was tiny. I slid on my stomach down the hall so I could hear what the two men in suits were saying. They talked about one of our members who owned a store and had moved to Carlsbad from Cincinnati, Ohio, before the union strike. Come to find out, according to the men in suits, who happened to be FBI agents, he was suspected to be a communist and the union, they said, had ties to him. Our leading church member was the president of the union. These were the days of Joe McCarthy, a well-known anti-communist senator from Wisconsin.

Stuff like that made no difference to me, and I had no idea what a communist was. Only by watching our Stromberg-Carlson black-and-white television and the TV show *I Led 3 Lives* did I have any knowledge of communism. My world extended barely further than the churchyard. All I knew was the store owner communist had a good-looking redheaded daughter in our church. For some reason, I kinda liked her, but the red hair made me pause.

Another girl named Barbara (she wasn't redheaded) was the first little girl I met when we moved to Carlsbad. My mama took me to an old ladies' missionary circle meeting (I was almost small enough to be her baby), and Barbara was there. Sixth grade. She was a pretty little thing, the daughter of that lady who went to the altar all the time—bless her heart. She had a little brother who pestered us. His mother would stay at the altar for hours on end and just couldn't quite get over her problems.

We moved to Carlsbad after the school year started, late November or the first part of December 1949. I came into the sixth grade midway through the year after kids had already known each other from growing up in Carlsbad, and I was the new kid on the block. In truth, I was a sixth-grade kid with the maturity of a first grader. That didn't go over too well with some of the boys, especially when we were playing kickball—no one knew what soccer was back then.

Playing kickball was a perfect time for one of the bully boys to come up behind me, saying, "I've been waiting a long time to do this!"

I was a brand-new kid, only at school for a few days, so I didn't know what he meant, and then he hit me upside the head. Didn't matter, 'cause I didn't know what conflict was, or meanness, or hate, or fighting. That moment was the first time I understood conflict and bullying in a meaningful way, and I got acquainted with my deep anger. It didn't take long for me to find out, because I was a new kid, and I was much smaller than everyone else, with a disfigured nose to boot.

Music Lifted Me

I learned to adapt and fit in by joining the band. My musical ability was . . . interesting. I jumped into everything, even when I didn't know what I was doing. It never hurt to try. I had no natural talent, but I didn't care. Looking back, did I have ADHD? Maybe I was trying to satisfy a deep hunger in my soul, trying to pull myself out of the quicksand of life.

I soon learned how to play the alto horn, trumpet, cornet, French horn, and baritone—they all had the same fingering, except the French horn required fingering with the left hand. I also took piano lessons, and then organ lessons, paid for by my mama. She was the janitor of the church, earning $2.50 a week, and the work she did was back-breaking.

You may recall that my mama's family had money, and that my parents inherited property in Texas with valuable mineral rights. In theory, it would have been easy for my parents to tap into those funds to pay for a few of life's niceties, like music lessons. Yes, I suppose they could have done so, but they didn't. And why not? Taking even a small portion of that away was unthinkable. And second, my parents both believed in the sanctity of hard work. Through labor and the fruit of labor, we are made stronger in mind and body. We have no higher calling than doing God's work, and so my mama's toils in that church to earn money for my piano lessons gave greater meaning to both her life and mine. The hardships we endured were by choice, and looking back, I believe they helped make me the person I became. I took no meal for granted, I wore my clothes until they were threadbare, and I worked hard to learn the piano because I knew they came at an enormous cost and sacrifice. But even now, I cry thinking about my mama sweeping and mopping and dusting. She was a saint!

The lady across the street taught piano, so she became my teacher. She smoked and had a daughter who could play the piano well. Her daughter was made fun of because she was extra heavy. We were both bullied, so we kinda went together.

My piano teacher helped me win a singing contest traveling to Roswell (known as the site of a UFO crash in 1947) to the first and only TV station in that part of New Mexico. Her daughter played the piano, and I sang. Nat King Cole's song, "Too Young," was popular back then, so I chose it to sing on TV in Roswell. There wasn't an *American Idol* or big-time TV, so some people came into town and asked kids to go to the hotel and audition. There I was—ready to sing.

Why they chose me, I'll never know. The next thing I knew, I was on my way to Roswell. I didn't win the whole state of New Mexico, but they made a little record of me singing. I had a real high voice since my voice had not changed yet. Didn't matter.

Fighting Mad

I was getting used to losing, and being bullied, too. Always, always, when I walked down the hall at school, bigger guys would find it necessary to push or shove me into the lockers, knock me down, or push me around in the restroom.

Sinking sand!

You gotta remember, I was only four feet, eleven inches tall and weighed ninety-eight pounds when I graduated from high school, so you know I was tiny from sixth grade to twelfth grade! When I was fourteen years old, going into ninth grade, my dad was five feet six and a muscular two hundred pounds; his hands and bones were enormous. Mama was five feet one. I had to wear jeans from the children's department but still rolled the pants up to keep them from dragging on the ground.

I'm not sure, but I think some of my activities were plain stupid simply because I was trying to lift myself up and out of my hurts. It didn't work. My music teacher had an evergreen tree out back with some tall grass around it. Their daughter and I had an idea that we could burn the grass. It didn't work. When the tree burned, we tried— tried—to put it out with the hose. Sorry, Charlie! Our intentions were good, but stupidity took control. She got in trouble, but I didn't, because I never told my folks. If I did, I knew Daddy would whup me, and the razor strop hurt real bad.

To this day, I think of another girl, Dora Mae, who lived directly across the street from us. Their house was so small you would think it was a shack. It was! She didn't have a mother, just a dad, and he worked in the mines. I always wondered how she felt with no mother. And I also wondered why they moved to Carlsbad from Mattoon, Illinois. She had rotten teeth and turned red when someone talked to her. I felt so sorry for her. She seemed terribly sad, and I wondered if her dad was taking advantage of her, because she had to do everything—cook, clean, wash clothes—everything. From time to time, she asked Mama if she could wash clothes at our house.

Dora Mae always sat on their crumbling front steps and stared out at whatever was there. Lonely. I always gravitated to the downtrodden, the lonely, the hurting, maybe because that's the way I felt deep inside. She started going to our church on the corner of Tenth and Fox. I hope it helped her and that she found hope and peace.

I didn't have any girlfriends who would admit I was their boyfriend because I had that thing in my nose, and besides, I was half everyone's size. Once again, I learned the art of adapting. If Carlsbad had had gangs, I probably would have joined. Come to think of it, there was a Mexican gang called the Pachucos, and they tattooed little crosses on their hand between the thumb and forefinger. That was OK and down my alley. Although I didn't have a horse anymore, I thought of myself as a cowboy and didn't know what gangs were.

On the east side of New Mexico, the high school football and basketball teams were outstanding—Carlsbad (Yeah! Cavemen!), Hobbs, Artesia, Roswell, Portales, and Clovis. The Cavemen even played against Odessa, Texas (Friday Night Lights) for a scrimmage, and people went out and cheered.

Sports didn't matter to me; they made me sad and angry, which was fine in my family. Daddy and Mama always tried to do the right thing, and they learned from the higher-ups that all sports were *bad*. Sinful. Probably as bad as a woman wearing lipstick and gold. On the other hand, as hobbies were concerned, music was encouraged. I was halfway good on the alto horn and pretty good on the French horn—alto for marching and French for orchestra. I had to get a letter from my folks to be excused from marching in the band at games because it was sinful.

After a while, I got tired of being bullied, and I got tired of sinking sand! One day I was out on the Pecos River (such as it was) trying to be accepted as one of the kids. My folks had no idea I was there. A big bully pushed me down in the water, and I thought I was going to drown. When I got out on the dry ground, spitting and coughing, I screamed and yelled, calling him dirty names, using as many cuss words as I knew. I didn't know many. I was probably a little over four feet tall, and he was maybe six feet tall. He came out of the water cussing, and I thought he was going to beat me up. Instead, something happened inside me, and I blindly swung my left fist—I'm left-handed. He wasn't expecting a left hand. It caught him on his right cheekbone, knocking him flat on his back. He was surprised, and I was in shock. He lurched up, and I ran like a jackrabbit. When I saw him at school, the side of his face was purple, yellow, and green with a bloodred eye. I was scared out of my wits, but he didn't bother me again.

My daddy always told me never to start a fight, but if someone starts a fight with me, finish it quickly! From that point on, a different kind of quicksand appeared around me, and destructive changes entered my heart and mind. A fit of absolute, liberating rage consumed my mind, which moved me to train for Golden Gloves boxing. I went all the way to state in the 112 lb. (and below) division, then lost. I'm not quite sure why my folks thought boxing was OK but football and basketball were not. Maybe it was because of Joe Louis, Ezzard Charles, and Rocky Marciano. Logic didn't seem to be an integral part of church life in the 1950s. Our behavior was based more on the dictates of higher church authorities and of the church Manual than on common sense and Bible exegesis.

My aunt Leona and uncle Rube lived in Carlsbad, and he was a cop. He wasn't a beer drinker, but he made sure all us kids got whatever we needed, especially Schlitz. I thought sinking sand was fun for a while, but it seemed I had to hide everything. I lied my way here and there, hoping my folks wouldn't find out—what a shame. My childlike innocence faded away.

In physical education, the teacher taught dancing. We had sock hops.

"Ooh, Marshall Hall, what would Jesus think?" said my aunt Leona.

I didn't tell Mama and Daddy, but I went because I didn't want kids to make fun of me for bringing in an excuse from my folks for religious reasons. They already made fun of me when I brought a written excuse for football and basketball games. I lived in mortal fear that someone would see me dancing and tell my daddy.

As a preacher's kid (PK), I was supposed to set the standard for the other kids, so early on, I became acutely sensitive to, "What will other people think?"

It was often whispered as one word. "*Whatwillotherpeoplethink?*"

I lived right on the edge between getting a whipping and acting out. While other kids went to get saved again on Sunday nights, I sat in the back of the church either carving my initials on the pew or making fun of reading songs in the songbook, adding, "between the sheets," like "amazing grace, between the sheets." You guessed it, Sunday nights were for getting saved again and again and again. Could never figure that out.

After I hit that bully down on the Pecos River, you would think I would have a little confidence, wouldn't you? Well, I did, but destructively. I developed a kind of deep anger that said, "I'm as mad as hell, and I ain't a-gonna take it anymore!" Know what I mean?

My lashing out came from both rage and insecurity. Boiling inside were the memories of kids making fun of that thing in my nose, of ol' Sister Horn, of whuppings, of bullies, of not being allowed to go to football games, of losing my happiness—all exacerbated by more conflict with bigger kids. They wanted to see what I had in me. I sneaked off and smoked real cigarettes (not cedar bark with Sears and Roebuck catalog paper) and drank beer. I liked Schlitz. Still, it all amounted to sinking sand. No one, I thought, could rescue me.

I couldn't go to games, but I could fight. No one could quite prepare for that left hand.

One day, the Robinson kid pushed me from behind and claimed that I had stolen his ballpoint pen, which I had not! His dad was a dentist in town, I think, and Daddy belonged to some kind of a service club with him. The Robinson kid grabbed me by the shoulder. I don't know how, but my reaction was automatic.

I turned and hit him in what I thought was my favorite spot.

I missed and hit him in the mouth, and out flew blood and teeth. His daddy told my daddy, and I thought for sure I was gonna get another whipping with the razor strop. But I didn't, and that made me feel good deep inside. For the first time, I felt like Daddy was proud of me, I guess. Daddy knew I had a problem. Still, I was sinking and sinking fast—on the edge.

Lost and Alone in the Desert

Seeking fun and fitting in with my peers frequently put me at odds with my parents and the church. Some of the kids liked to go out into the hills surrounding Carlsbad, exploring the many caverns deep underground (Carlsbad is known for the caverns). We explored that whole area for recreation. Always, always, I had to lie to go anywhere. It became a pattern of behavior to lie.

"What will other people think?"

My folks were the most admirable people in the world, but for some reason, I could never tell them anything. Kids just didn't do that back in those days. So I sank more and more into a world of secret hurts.

Traveling with the school band to Chihuahua, Mexico, was the experience of my lifetime. We went there because President Eisenhower had a program called "People to People International," and somehow, they chose us to represent the USA. We got kicked out of Mexico because some of the kids got drunk (not me), and getting drunk was a no-no. When we returned, the school called all the parents into the auditorium and tattled on us. I didn't get a whipping this time. My daddy was born in 1898, and kids back in those days were whipped, not spanked—"spare the rod, spoil the child." But by that time, I guess my folks were just exhausted trying to straighten me out.

As a teenager in Carlsbad, I engaged in activities such as playing cowboys and Indians by shooting BB guns at other kids with BB guns, but I was never happy. The abuse I suffered as a five- or six-year-old started boiling inside, and I had no idea what was wrong with me. I wet the bed until I was fourteen years old. The inner rage finally caught up with me, shaped by the child I once was, damaged, incapable of intimacy. Relationships were not my thing.

Nevertheless, I yearned for a friend or friends who could lift me out of the sinking sand, someone who could heal my heart. After about the age of six, I became a scared child, scared and angry. I was afraid enough to lie my way to achievement. Psychologists could probably analyze this as a fight-or-flight response.

Throughout my life, I have always been able to detect this rage in others. It's now instinctual, akin to having danger lift the hair on the back of my neck, as when a wild animal or a mean dog comes close. I don't care if that person professes to be as holy-moly as the queen of Scotland—I can sense it. Some may act super sweet and kind, but I instinctively know to be careful. Don't mess with them. They are gentle on the outside, but "I'm gonna eat you alive" on the inside.

The old-timers in the church preached about "that root of bitterness," "the old nature," and "original sin." Have you seen some church people act angry, disturbed, or just plain mean? I have. I detected it through intuition, telepathy, or something way out there.

Arrogant? I know it when I see it.

Ungenuine? Yes, I can detect this, too.

This inner enlightenment was a blessing and a curse all my adult life. At first, I questioned these strange feelings. Soon, I came to accept them when, time after time and instance after instance, they were proven correct. It's a superpower I almost wish I didn't have, because I know it comes from great suffering.

One day while in junior high school, I took my canteen and wandered around in the desert hills outside of Carlsbad. Soon my water was gone in the intense summer heat. I was lost. I hallucinated. Stumbling around, I climbed to the highest hill nearby, looking for a town or someone to help. I saw nothing but more desert—no water, despite being thirstier than I had ever known. Fortunately, I remembered some things I learned in scouting. I took my knife and cut into a cactus. Although the water was somewhat slimy, it sustained me until I could find my way home.

Years later, while reading Matthew 5:6, my experience in the desert vividly brought to life the words of Jesus, "Blessed are they which do hunger and thirst after righteousness: for they shall be filled." Many have faced life's sufferings, creating a deep soul hunger or thirst for the Savior.

In John 4, Jesus went to the village well, and a lower-class woman was there. In the culture of the day, a Jew would not be caught dead talking to a Samaritan woman, but Jesus asked her for a drink. She must have been shocked and embarrassed, because Jesus saw it on her face. To paraphrase, He said, "If you only knew what God has waiting for you, you would ask me, and I would give you water that will last for a lifetime." They talked back and forth because she just couldn't understand. Too many questions!

Then Jesus clarified by saying people get thirsty again and again after drinking water from the well. In John 4:14, He said, "But the water that I shall give him shall be in him a well of water springing up into everlasting life." The woman had never heard of this mysterious spiritual cleansing. Oh boy! Her misunderstanding set her off, because she brought up everything from hither to yon: (1) Give me the water, and I won't have to make this trip all the time; (2) I don't have a husband, and what does that matter anyway? (3) I've had five husbands and the one now, oh well; (4) What about the Jews? (5) Is Jerusalem the only place to worship? (6) My ancestors taught me this and that.

Tapping into Christian spiritual principles is not always an easy step, especially when one has no previous understanding or teaching.

When one is delirious in heart and mind, the pain can wipe out the ability to understand, to feel, to analyze. Even those closest to Jesus could not fathom spiritual concepts, prompting Jesus to ask in Matthew 16:13, "Whom do men say that I the Son of man am?"

To the Samaritan woman, Jesus knew exactly what to say. No, He didn't argue or debate. He simply said in John 4:21–24 that the time was coming when all her questions would be like water running off a duck's back:

> Jesus saith unto her, Woman, believe me, the hour cometh, when ye shall neither in this mountain, nor yet at Jerusalem, worship the Father. Ye worship ye know not what: we know what we worship: for salvation is of the Jews. But the hour cometh, and now is, when the true worshippers shall worship the Father in spirit and in truth: for the Father seeketh such to worship Him. God is a Spirit: and they that worship Him must worship Him in spirit and in truth.

She said she knew all this, but everything would be OK only after the Messiah arrived.

And Jesus put it right down in front of her in John 4:26: "I that speak unto thee am He."

No misunderstanding there!

At last, I understood how I survived that harrowing day in the desert.

Some tough kids I knew said that they were going to run away from home, and I said I would go, too. I hungered to be relieved and free from the hurt and anger inside. It didn't have anything to do with Mama and Daddy, because our home was happy. It was that sinking feeling! Anyway, the word got out, and Daddy caught me before we left. Those other boys were arrested in Kilgore, Texas, and thrown in jail. That near-runaway experience did nothing for my shredded heart. I hurt so bad all the time.

The sinking sands of insecurity, immaturity, inferiority, rejection, and bullying caused me to take Daddy's long rifle Springfield 22 and hold it to my mouth. I was too small to reach the trigger; I never thought to use my toe. I guess something stopped me, and it didn't happen. Deep down where only I lived, the pain of my soul burdened my immature heart. I don't think I had ever had a genuine spiritual experience. Sitting in church, having wonderful Christian parents, living in a minister's home—nothing seemed to pull me out of the sinking sand. Because I wallowed in the basement of my soul, I developed empathy for so many others who carry their own demons.

Odd Jobs

Somewhat later, perhaps a year, the new owner of a drugstore across the street from the high school needed a soda jerk, so I applied. Why did he hire me? Probably because my daddy was a preacher. He probably figured I'd be responsible if nothing else. I was to cook hamburgers, make sandwiches, dip ice cream cones, pour cokes, and make sure the kids didn't mess up the jukebox.

Do you remember the diner in *Happy Days*, the TV show that aired in the seventies? Well, it was like that. We had no McDonald's or Burger King in town but, good news, shortly after that, someone put in an A&W restaurant. Up to that time, no franchises existed in Carlsbad, and the only other one that came our way, eventually, was Dairy Queen.

A guy named Cecil was a member of our church, and he taught our junior high Sunday school class. He's the guy who caught us smoking cigars when we went on a class outing. He was also the assistant manager of the J. C. Penney Company. He hired me to work as a window dresser and interior designer. Other high school kids would pass the window along the street while I was dressing the models and point at me. Before long, I decided to put up sheets over the window so no one could see me. Cecil taught me well. Then along came Safeway, where I worked filling grocery bags, and then a little after that, the local funeral home hired me. My big brother, Martin Luther, worked there a few years before. *Wow!* Talk about a variety of experiences.

Life on the Edge

People didn't talk about ADHD in the 1950s. In my family, we just existed by going to church. Bitterness and my hurting heart never came up. Our family gathered from time to time at the parsonage, and Mama cooked the best food, pinto beans and all. Martin Luther and Joy (with kids Edward and Joana), Nantha Lee and Lloyd (with kids Elaine and Ronnie), and Howard Phillip and one of his many wives (Jean) and his daughter (Glenna) all lived in Carlsbad at the same time for a while. Eventually, Nantha Lee moved to Ventura, California, where she took up making hairpieces for men, an art form she got so good at that she even made them for celebrities like Frank Sinatra. Martin Luther later moved to Abilene, Texas, in 1959 and worked for Ford dealers selling cars and trucks for a while until he got into property management and development.

Howard Phillip had about seven wives. His first one was a Cisco girl named Louise. They separated once, but while they were together, they had one child (Glenna) the first time and a son the second time. The other wives are a mystery. When he moved to Carlsbad, he brought another wife (Jean) home from San Diego; at least we assumed she was his wife. She had a pest of a little boy, and he was always getting into things.

My brother, Martin Luther, was preparing to take us hunting the next day and had a Browning .30-06 rifle I was to use. We were all in the kitchen, and Martin Luther was showing me how to use it. Unfortunately, he mistakenly left a round in it. That little pest of a kid—Jean's kid—constantly looked down the barrel, and everybody kept pulling him and yelling at him to get away.

Nevertheless, he kept it up. Then he ran over in front of the gun again. Howard yanked him away, and a split second later, the gun went off and blew a big hole in the kitchen sink, through the cabinet, and out the wall of the house. The bullet wound up in the concrete retaining wall, or what was left of it, by the church. The sound was deafening! All of us were in god-awful shock! No one moved or said anything for at least a full sixty seconds. The blood drained from all our faces. We just stood there, no one moving. By the grace of God, our whole family was protected from a devastating life change.

A few weeks later, I went with a bunch of kids into the hills, way high up to where a spring with fresh water came out of the ground. The water ran down over green moss, on and on. Being a natural explorer, I was enticed to find out where the water went. As I ran, the water cooled my feet in the hot New Mexico sun. Then I encountered the hundred-foot cliff. I slid on my feet, then, falling on my side, I grasped for anything that could hold me. The slick green moss provided no purchase. I tumbled over a small rise in the rock. I screamed—to no avail! Then something—someone—stopped my slide. As I looked over the edge, I knew.

I. Just. Knew!

I suspect you could remember times when God intervened in your life as well.

I learned something valuable from that experience. Sometimes, but not always, God protects us from our stupidity. God always forgives our sins, but in many if not most cases, the consequences of our sins and ignorance will bring suffering for years to come.

When I was in my junior or senior year in high school, stupidity raised its ugly head. Stupidity was no stranger to me; in fact, I still do a few stupid things. Maybe this is because I do stuff before I think. I heard about the church in Alamogordo, New Mexico, needing volunteers to install flooring in the sanctuary.

I can do that, I thought.

On the weekend, some friends and I drove home from Alamogordo to Carlsbad. We stopped in Artesia to see a friend. Driving through the mountains in my 1954 Chevrolet, I enjoyed sliding around the corners. But it was sprinkling, and the highway was slick.

Yep, you guessed it.

I crashed into the side of the mountain and over a thirty-five-foot embankment, not quite straight down. A cable caught the right rear tire housing, and we dangled over the edge! Three scared teenagers, white as sheets. We dared not move a muscle!

Would you believe it, a guy with a tow truck saw the whole thing! He attached a line to my car, and after about an hour, we were on our way again. The side of my car looked like it had been through World War II and was terribly out of alignment. By the time we reached Artesia, the vehicle was undrivable—oil draining and all the rubber worn off the left front tire. Daddy had to come rescue us; it wasn't a pretty picture. Daddy shook his head, pursed his lips, and took a deep breath.

Wake-Up Call at Church Camp

Those harrowing experiences in Carlsbad finally sank in. Enough of that! Life isn't all bad when you have a praying mom and dad, because you can count on intervention from God's angels through His Holy Spirit, although He gave us free will. Even when it seems that life is like someone stomping on your head, "He looks beyond our faults and sees our need."

> I shall forever lift mine eyes to Calvary,
> To view the cross where Jesus died for me.
> How marvelous the grace that caught my falling soul.
> He looked beyond my faults and saw my need.
> (Dottie Rambo, "He Looked Beyond My Faults," 1967)

Thank God for church camp. Daddy bought a brand-new 1956 aqua-green-and-white Plymouth, four doors, one of those newfangled ones that had buttons for gearshifts. Wow! All you had to do was push a button that said *D*, and it would go forward.

Daddy, Mama, and I packed it all up and headed for church camp outside Capitan, New Mexico. By this time, I was seventeen years old, had just graduated from high school, didn't know where I was going to college, had the maturity of a twelve-year-old, and was as lost as a goose. Who cared at that point? It didn't matter, because Daddy let me drive the car out of Carlsbad, north through Artesia, into Roswell, turning left on US Route 380, past Ruidoso, and on to the camp between Ruidoso and Capitan.

Mount Baldy was on our left, and Mama kept saying, "Marshall Hall, you watch the road, don't look up there."

I guess Daddy was resigned to think if I did something stupid, oh well, it wouldn't be the first time. The camp was nestled way high in the mountains. The drive and sights were great.

I pulled off the asphalt and started up the winding dirt road into the camp. Rain speckled the windshield. We were early—we always were. Being early for everything was in our DNA, although no one knew what DNA was back in those days. As I pulled carefully up the rocky, gravelly road, a little old lady (maybe fifty years old) the wife of the camp maintenance man, was standing in the way, crying and waving her hands. To the left stood a wrecked tractor, one that had a blade on the back and a shovel on the front. Her husband had his head caught between the forks of a tree. He had probably bounced around on the tractor, going too fast, up and over as on a trampoline. Gone. Dead. My mother, always full of compassion, hugged the man's wife, comforting her as Daddy moved the tractor.

That campground was later to be the site of many other catastrophes. In 1965, a cabin fell on Dr. R. C. Gunstream, the New Mexico district superintendent of Bonita Park, and killed him. A small fire during youth camp brought all of us out into the cold night, passing bucket after bucket of water along to splash on the burning cabins (I think three in all). In 2012, the most significant forest fire in New Mexican history destroyed the whole campground, about 150 acres of beautiful forestland. I would imagine that more than two hundred structures were destroyed, burned to the ground. All told, the fire consumed about two hundred thousand acres of New Mexican forest, three hundred square miles. You can read about it in the news. Mercy!

A lot of good things happened there, too. We played during the day and had church services at night. The singing was excellent. Listening to the pastors' wives play evangelistically on the piano was wonderfully uplifting. When the preacher asked if anyone wanted to come forward and pray, my daddy came back to me, crying, and asked if I would go to the altar. I shook my head, no. But just as he turned to leave, deep down in my heart, something, someone, spoke to me.

I said to myself, *It's time.*

There and then, on July 4, 1956, for the first time in my life, I made a conscious decision, and sure enough, Christ "looked beyond my faults and saw my need." No words can explain the overpowering relief and joy I had in knowing the indwelling Christ, His presence, and His forgiveness.

No more shifting or sinking sand, I mistakenly thought. *Solid rock,* I guessed. But boy-oh-boy, another battle began, this time on a spiritual level!

This new battle was and has been fierce and peculiarly rigorous—fear, insecurity, uncertainty, stupidity, guilt, sin, rejection, distrust, and, of course, Satan's constant roadblocks, deceits, and accusations. At first, I thought I would never be stupid again. Unfortunately, it didn't work that way. My life became a series of battles, victory after victory, loss after loss.

But I could never get straight that forgiveness comes *before* behavior, not after! I couldn't get this through my thick head. Honestly, I always thought I had to quit being stupid and behave first, then God would be happy with me, and I would go to heaven.

How heartbreaking!

We must believe and trust first (ask forgiveness, repent), then we are born into the family of God through Jesus. Another Gaither song, "When He Was on the Cross," plays in my mind when I recall the moment. At this point, I was like a baby just learning to walk. Read about it in Romans 4. It certainly took me a while to get over stupidity!

Moving Yet Again

By that time in Carlsbad, our church became the First Church of the Nazarene because the union guys wanted their own church, so they convinced the DBS to let them start one. That was all right, I guess, because someone said that the Baptists grow from splits and divisions, and if they can do it, so can the little fish. One preacher said that church growth for Baptists in those days was like hearing two cats fighting late at night. Screeching and scratching like a real fight, then a couple of months later, a whole new litter of kittens is born. I could never understand this.

By this time, it seemed Carlsbad had the makings of a long-term, stable home life. I had a few friends, I felt happy, and I even started to grow—physically. Of course, I was still uncommonly small for someone my age, but half an inch seemed to come out of nowhere, and pretty soon, I didn't feel quite so tiny. But then it was time for me to go to college.

In my dreams, I wanted to go to the University of New Mexico, but my high school grades were horrible, just horrible, and I had no chance of being accepted had I even applied. Instead, I went to a church college, which I thought was going to be like a celestial church camp. It wasn't!

One day, my parents dropped me off on Route 66 in Oklahoma City to start a new life as a college student at Bethany Nazarene College, now Southern Nazarene University. A new chapter began.

8

College

Maturity matters. Not everyone should be forced into certain social and educational requirements based on age. Being tyrannized by immaturity and oppressed by subpar educational experiences stunts social development. Add the ecclesiastical element, and it seems to be the yin and yang of personal growth.

I stood on the curb of Highway 66, watching my folks drive away, crying. Yeah, it affected me a little bit, but I was a grown-up now—free as a bird! Mama and Daddy enrolled me in college, and I had a roommate in Fanning Hall. Things were exciting. I had become a Christian, so I thought, and this was like heaven to me without crossing over the Jordan.

It was heaven until I remembered that I was me, and people are people. Geological solid rock is not absolutely stable. Nothing on this earth is. Changes in temperature, expansion and contraction, and movements deep in the ground all present an imperfect picture. It may be stable compared to something else, but nothing, absolutely nothing on this earth, is perfect. Elliptical flaws or cracks permeate all rocks. Even El Capitan of Yosemite National Park expands and contracts, leaving slight cracks that some say could cause it to break away a million years from now "if the creek don't rise and the Lord don't come," as Hank Williams used to say.

I was on the Solid Rock, more particularly, Christ the Solid Rock. No flaws mar this Rock. *Christ doesn't change,* I thought. If so, where was that childlike joy and happiness I sometimes knew as a little guy? Where were those days of purity, hope, innocence, and acceptance? I thought I would become a solid rock like my daddy and my mama. Still, it didn't feel that way when I walked in the front door of the college in Bethany, Oklahoma, one beautiful, warm afternoon in August 1956.

Kids and people from all walks of life and all backgrounds were at that college. Some kids had come from pastors' homes, big shots' homes, blue-collar homes, alcoholics' homes. Some had been to another college. Some were older, having had adult experiences. Some were innocent, savvy, former military guys, mature and immature, big, little, great, and small. Everyone brought their flaws. Some had been Christians for a long time, and some weren't Christians at all. For the most part, other than a few arrogant and snooty ones, everyone was friendly.

Here I was all saddled up and religioned, ready to enjoy church college camp or college church camp, whatever. I was a dry sponge wanting to be liked, wanting to participate, wanting to achieve, wanting to be a part of something. What I didn't realize in my imma-ture mind at eighteen was: (a) this was a college, not a church camp; (b) this was root hog or die; (c) no one was going to bow down and call me blessed; (d) I was still me with all my flaws, problems, disappoint-ments, and stupidities; and (e) I was a new Christian, like a newborn baby trying to ambulate through my first few years of Christian life, crying, falling, and pooping my communal and spiritual pants.

Growing up, my mama cleaned, washed, and ironed my clothes, teaching me to do the same. Fanning Hall was a piece of you-know-what, like living in the ghetto. Two weeks was enough for me.

I need a job, I thought.

Back to Work

Yep, I needed a job. When my big brother went to this same college, he worked at a funeral home down the street. From there, he went to embalming college in Dallas and married. Since he had experience with dead people, he got a job immediately. And he was a big guy out of the military.

Guess what I did? I marched my four-foot, eleven-and-a-half-inch frame right down the street, an eighteen-year-old housed in a twelve-year-old mind and body, and told the funeral home they needed me to work there. Bill Merritt, the owner, promptly got rid of me by referring me to a brand-new funeral home on Capitol Hill, south of downtown Oklahoma City, that did double-duty providing local ambulance service. It was a nice way of pawning me off. I got the job and lived in the basement below the embalming room.

If you have never had to walk up black-as-pitch stairs at 2:00 a.m., open the door to an embalming room, feel along the wall for the light, smell embalming fluid, and be jerked awake by the sight of two dead people on slabs when you just needed to go to the bathroom, then I would recommend trying it. You won't need to watch horror films anymore to get that jolt. Real life abruptly spoke to me! Thinking of my mortality did not affect me, but observing the dead with all the sights and smells jerked me backward through a knothole.

Since the owner of the funeral home was my boss, he made sure I had the experience of a lifetime. I was the lowest guy on the totem pole. One day we were called out to a "poor farm," a place where the county kept old men who could no longer take care of themselves. I thought we were going to a home to take someone to the hospital. Not so. When we arrived, it looked more like a flophouse.

The director of the place told us to get our gurney (or something that could be taken way out into the pasture where the cows were). He gathered about six or eight of his guys, and we trekked through weeds and trees, down a ravine, up the other side, and through some more trees, pulling the gurney until the director said, "Over there."

We walked about another fifty feet, and lying on the ground was the body of an old man. On the tree under which he lay was tied a red bandana and a broken rope. I have no idea what the red bandana was for. But the old boy lay dead as a doornail. He must have been there a couple of days or so, maybe four. The smell even made my boss put his handkerchief over his face.

We knew what to do—pick the guy up and put him on the gurney! Simple. I lifted the upper arms and my boss lifted the legs. The deceased man was beginning to decay. I didn't like this, but I was an employee doing what I was supposed to do, so I bent down, staring the old guy in the face, and reached down to lift. As I lifted, my fingers broke through the cloth and into rotten flesh. All the guys standing around, including my boss, laughed their rear ends off. They knew I was the sucker. Right then and there, I knew I wasn't cut out to be a funeral home employee. Forget the money! And besides, I had a sensitive nose. I'm not sure why I didn't quit that day, but for some reason, I stayed with it a while longer.

Since funeral homes usually had the ambulance services in Oklahoma City (OKC), the owner of this one made a bid for the county contract so that all emergencies and welfare cases came to us. I wasn't allowed to drive the ambulance. I don't think my legs were long enough to reach the accelerator or brake. The owner drove until things got so busy, he hired another guy. The other guy was about twenty-five years old. One day he and I carried a three-hundred-pound, beat-up drunk man down three flights of narrow stairs. Another time, I picked a man's head off the road after an automobile accident. And, yes, I cried when we conducted funerals, but I had to get over that crying stuff. Funeral directors were to be "professional." Although I had the appearance of a child, I was supposed to be somber, helpful, and sympathetic.

My most poignant experience was a call late one night to go to the bottom of the city ghetto where a lady was in the midst of having a baby. We drove to a one-room shack built with old Coca-Cola signs. It had a dirt floor, and four or five wide-eyed little kids stood around. A single light bulb hung from the ceiling, and the diseased mother with sores all over her lower body was lying on rags with the top of a baby's head peeking out. My helper guy saw it and ran outside, vomiting.

I was scared to death. The mother was awake, almost catatonic. I thought I might catch a disease from her, but a sense of compassion came over me, so I dove right in and got that little sucker out, holding him in my arms just as a county doctor showed up. I had no idea what the thing hanging out of the baby's stomach was. I just stood there, fighting tears. We didn't know what rubber gloves were back then. The doctor took over, and my heart was crushed, looking at those poor little kids standing there in shock. I've often wondered what happened to those kids.

The Wrong Sort of Companions

After about six weeks, I finally quit my job at the funeral home. I got tired of going to the bathroom through the embalming room, and I figured if I didn't get away from dead people, I was going to die myself. My folks had already spent $1,500 (about $15,000 in 2020) on tuition, room and board, clothes, and other expenses in just a couple of months of college. It wasn't that I didn't care or wasn't appreciative; I was too goofy and immature to grasp the importance of building a life. So I moved my stuff back to the college, Chapman Hall, in the third or fourth week of October 1956. Can you believe that all this stuff happened in the first two months or so of my college career?

My first roommate at Chapman Hall was a good ol' boy from western Kansas, a farm boy. Was he low class, common, or blue collar? Absolutely not. He flew his Beechcraft Bonanza airplane down and parked it out with the Aero Commanders. Rich. Definitely out of my financial and intellectual league. He later went to graduate school for a law degree at an Ivy League university (Cornell). He became president of a large, international corporation associated with two billionaire guys out of Wichita, Kansas, whose names you would recognize. He made something of himself, but he still wasn't one of the elites on campus. Gotta remember, a pecking order exists in every organization.

Two "in" groups thrived on the college campus. I was not part of either group, and neither was my roommate. I was just a kid attending "church" camp. The first anointed "in" group was made up of the upper intelligentsia (I assumed they thought of themselves as being above everybody else). Not all of the smart or wealthy were accepted. One member of this group even ran for president of the United States, Gary Hart—he changed his name from Gary Hartpence because it sounded like "hot pants."

Others of this first group thought the Nazarenes were below their caste, so they joined up with a higher class of ecclesiastical clergy and theologians that later attended East Coast seminaries like Andover Newton and universities like Yale. The second group usually had a kind of church connection—their dads were either big shots or they were dating sons or daughters of big shots. Many of these church-connected kids already knew each other. Both of the above two groups were privileged. I admired them, but they were definitely out of my league, or more accurately, they were above my league. What they thought of me, if they thought of me at all, was probably that I was clueless. I had so little life experience, they must've thought of me as a small puppy dog, hanging around for who knew what reason.

It didn't take me long to meet people, because I thought I was at church camp. Also, I was "saved," and I thought everyone else was, too. Soon after moving to the campus, I heard about boxing in the basement of Fanning Hall. These guys were big. Everybody was big except me, but this was a way I could be accepted. I wasn't and never would be invited into that illustrious collection of "in" groups, so I volunteered to box anybody and everybody. Most felt sorry for me, but they all underestimated my speed and power and soon got whupped. Some I even knocked out. But these were common, ordinary guys. They were not the intelligentsia. Fighting them only served to put me on the lower level of the social ladder with them.

Another group of kids were children of missionaries. They were considered peculiar. They simply had personalities that didn't fit in. They were probably like other pastors' kids who didn't have friends growing up, like yours truly.

As I look back on those early experiences, Satan was using my flaws of insecurity, anger, and feelings of inferiority as an attempt to destroy me.

Oh, you don't have a full understanding that Satan is real and tries to destroy? He is called the destroyer and deceiver in the Bible. Better read Ephesians 6:12. "For we wrestle not against flesh and blood, but against principalities, against powers, against the rulers of the darkness of this world, against spiritual wickedness in high places."

Mama sent me to college with cuff links, tie tacks and ties, and white shirts, all fashionable clothes she purchased in the children's department. Being innocent and immature, I tagged on to an extremely strict group of "hal-lee-loo-yer" religious boys, or more particularly, they tagged on to me. To be accepted, I had to go to ten o'clock prayer meetings every night in the basement of the campus church. If I didn't, Jesus wouldn't love me, because I had to behave myself first, then He would be right there by my side.

Frequently I rode with this bunch to the Reno Street ghetto while they preached and sang on the street corner to the bums and homeless—negativity, criticism, word-for-word Bible reading, but club-like, and I desperately wanted to be accepted into a club. They criticized me if I wore a tie. Tie tacks were out; cuff links were assuredly a sin. This crazy stuff just about "rurned" me!

Kids in my college classes were unquestionably far above me in intellect and maturity. They all seemed to know each other while I knew no one. These kids already knew how to study. They knew how to do homework. Anger built up. Why? I thought I loved Jesus. I felt He had already forgiven me for being stupid, too. Was I gonna go through some sinking sand . . . again?

I felt bullied on a higher level—by arrogance, by rejection, by feelings of inferiority. I felt like a person to be avoided. The intelligentsia would not even acknowledge me. Maybe they didn't see me because I was so short. Of course, none of this was real. I know now these were stories I made up in my mind! We all tell ourselves such stories, but in the decades since, I've learned to turn them around by asking myself a simple question: "How do I know?"

By doing so, I forced my mind to look at the hard data instead of conclusions reached by an emotional sense of inferiority. I hope others may read this and learn from my mistake.

Music to My Ears

The college administration scheduled a fall revival around October or November, a time when they had big-name preachers and singers visit campus. Mercy me, I had never seen this before in my whole life. I knew I had discovered Christ, but college and the big church experience with a thousand kids were mind-blowing, almost hallucinatory. Great choirs, marvelous singing groups, and anointed preaching placed me in a celestial world of spiritual understanding I had never known before. I was still stupid in some of my behavior and felt left out of things. As my eyes opened, I rethought my position. Nope, this was not church camp.

How do I get over this? Why? Will I ever fit in? Will I ever be accepted by the spiritual and intellectual bourgeoisie?

During this purgatory of adjustment, an older guy who had been in the military suggested we go into Oklahoma City to a beatnik place. What? I had no idea what a beatnik place was. We went. Beatniks were in vogue before hippies. They sat around in dark coffee houses, wore French berets, played soft music, and someone would stand up and quote poetry or something and say, "The world is round," and all the people would fall into an intellectual trance. It was exciting, but I felt like a sinner when we left. Maybe it was the coffee; I don't know. I always felt like a sinner. Normal.

A few times, I met with different guys who liked to sing. Hey, I could sing! I could read music, too, and I could play the piano to a respectable degree. I loved to hear them practice, so a few times, I joined in. My voice had become extremely low, a bass, and it was funny having such a deep voice in a little bitty body. They called me the little man with a big voice.

One of the official college quartets lost their bass, and they needed one. Perfect—except I didn't fit the mold. I wasn't a part of the "in" crowd. Another guy who was in the "in" crowd, Ron Barlow, deserved the spot more than I. He could sing better, didn't have a thing in his nose, and was tall, handsome, and destined to be a prominent physician in the OKC area. He had even sung with the group a few times in public concerts. Now, who do you think they chose?

Come on. Be honest.

I was heartbroken. I prayed . . . more like wishing or bargaining, crying like a two-year-old and throwing a tantrum to myself. I held it all inside, as was my custom. Belial (which means "lacking worth"), Satan the destroyer, called me a loser, worthless. I knew I had discovered the only Solid Rock in the universe, but I was still stupid in some of my behavior. I couldn't pull myself out of the sand!

Opportunity literally knocked on my door, but I foolishly turned it away when a talented musician named Whitey Gleason contacted me because he heard I could sing bass. Basses and tenors were in short supply. He had a group that sang southern gospel quartet music like the Statesmen Quartet. Fantastic (although that word wasn't often used)! Whitey was an unbelievable pianist, arranger, singer, and songwriter. He wanted me to sing with them regularly, and if I had done so, I might have moved up in the southern gospel music business. Who knows? Later on, Whitey became the pianist for the big-time, nationally recognized quartet, The Blackwood Brothers.

Yet I turned him down. My heart was set on becoming a member of the college quartet . . . maybe, just maybe, although I had no illusions of grandeur.

Late one evening, Ron, the boy destined to be the bass member of the college quartet and the one who deserved the place more than I, asked me to meet him outside the basement door of the college church. I thought he simply wanted to express his sympathy and pat me on the head, and then I could go on living my undeserving, underdog life. He was a prince of a guy, gentle and courteous. To my surprise, he told me he planned to become a physician and that his study load would not permit him to do outside work. He eventually earned his MD and became Dr. Ron Barlow.

My heart fell in humble shame for the unwarranted anger I had toward him. Ron said he would recommend me to the standing quartet and the college administrators. He said they should choose me, which they subsequently did. I was to receive board, room, tuition, essential clothing, and other miscellaneous spending money, plus, we could sell and keep the money from our recordings. All told, this was valued at something over $25,000 per year today. Immediately after I went to the chapel and prayed, I called my parents.

Our group had not become well-known . . . yet. We had a vision, and as the Bible states in Proverbs 29:18, "Where there is no vision, the people perish." Deep in my inner self, I was being pulled out of the quicksand. I had not come to a place of self-sufficiency. In fact, I knew that my hope was "built on nothing less than Jesus's blood and righteousness." Edward Mote's hymn continues, "I dare not trust the sweetest frame, but wholly lean on Jesus's name."

I distanced myself from those strict, negative, "spiritual" boys not because I was doing other things but because that negativity came at an awful price. They thought I had backslid. Nazarene Christians didn't (and don't) believe in eternal security, making it a necessity to get saved over and over again, mostly on Sunday nights and revivals—I'm joking, of course. But living a judgmental life breeds a toxic attitude.

The college had never had a celebrity quartet before, that is, one that sang for all types of audiences in both church and secular venues. The closest they came was when a guy named Robert Hale sang in the group that represented the college. He later moved to New York for the Metropolitan Opera and Moscow, Russia, for the Goldovsky Opera. Later on, he teamed up with a guy named Dean Wilder, so they became Wilder 'n' Hale. I think they had to change their public relations name to Hale 'n' Wilder because Wilder 'n' Hale got too close to being "wilder than hell," and that just wouldn't do for church folks.

When our group first started in November 1956, we chose the name "The Collegiates." An English professor scolded me and said the correct usage should be "The Collegians." I never knew the difference and didn't care anyway. The name "The Collegiate Quartet" stuck, or maybe "The Collegiates." So what?

Left to right: Henry Cheatwood, Danny Steele, Dean Neff, and Marshall Pryor.

Day after day, we practiced and practiced and practiced. My life was built around the quartet, not academics. I had only been at the college since the middle of August 1956, so it seemed in my extremely immature mind that I was still attending church camp. The quartet consumed me, and nothing else mattered. Maybe this all-consuming passion is what helped me hide the wounds of my heart, immaturities, insecurities, and childhood guilt. Perhaps it was all about me.

These were the days of regional divisions in our church life. Some sections of the college territory were known as liberal (their lady members wore lipstick, wedding bands, and had bobbed hair), and others were known to be the true "spurtchual" ones. The women always took the harshest criticism if they didn't wear their hair in a bun. Mercy me! This was somewhat like the Fundamentalist Latter-Day Saints without the sex stuff (though there might have been a little of that, too).

When the Collegiate Quartet started singing songs like "Standing on the Corner Watching All the Girls Go By," and singing to service clubs, conventions, and hotels with a few cocktail lounges thrown in, some of the "spurtchual" groups lit up the sky with apocalyptic rumblings. Shortly after that, one of the DBSs (District Big Shots) left the church and started his own group. I rather doubt it was because of us standing on the corner watching the girls or singing "On the Street Where You Live" (from *Camelot*).

Education took a back seat. My first term paper—typed on my Smith Corona using onionskin paper with a thousand corrections— was given back to me with a large, red *C-minus* from the professor. Not to worry. I was an achiever by hook or crook. Just as in high school, my grades were horrible, terrible, a disgrace. Maybe the college dean didn't kick me out because of the quartet. It cost them a lot of money to keep me there. Perhaps the Lord had something to do with it.

After singing around the OKC area, our first big gig was to travel to Lawton, Oklahoma, to sing for a district banquet of Kiwanians at the Lawtonian Hotel. Probably more than seven hundred people were there. We did OK, but our performance was nothing to write home about. We continued to practice and travel, getting better and better. Our second tenor left, and another guy took his place. We got better with the new guy, Dean Neff—he looked and sang like Eddie Fisher— and expanded our portfolio of songs. After the summer of 1957 was over, the two middle guys, Dean Neff and Henry Cheatwood, second tenor and baritone, graduated, requiring us to search for two new members.

As I look back on this process of choosing, it was somewhat humor-ous. Leaders of the college administration, beholden to other leaders of the church, tried their best to force-feed a member on us, a relative-to-be of a "supreme" leader.

When we declined because he just couldn't sing, the college presi-dent wrung his hands in frightful anxiety and said, "What will Dr. So-and-So think?"

Amusing and amazing!

As it all came together, the two new guys we chose were talented beyond measure and easy to get along with. Danny Steele and I were the anchors at both ends of the quartet. Danny was a tenor, and I sang bass.

Confused as always, one day, I stopped by the dormitory chapel. No one was there. It didn't matter how much acclaim I received, how many times I heard the crowds clap or shout *amen*, or how many big shots I met, those childhood hurts and hates were still dogging me. I had no idea what I wanted to do with my life. My grades were horrendous. I was still small—about five foot three by now—and I still had that thing in my nose. It wouldn't have mattered if I was suddenly elevated to be the king of Siam. It just didn't matter. I knelt at the altar of the chapel, opened my Bible, and read 2 Timothy 4:2, "Preach the word; be instant in season, out of season; reprove, rebuke, exhort with all long suffering and doctrine."

If you can call me a theologian of sorts, I do not believe in the verbal inspiration of the Scriptures; that is, I do not believe that each word is to be taken literally from the Bible, leading one to do precisely as it says. I believe in the plenary inspiration of Scripture, taking the context surrounding the Scripture verse to find out what it means.

Therefore, from the moment I read those words in 2 Timothy, I didn't jump up and down, saying to myself, "Hallelujah, I'm called to preach!"

But I had a definite "knowing." From that time forward, I was sure! It had nothing to do with my family, my dad, or the Christian college I was attending. It had to do with an inner "calling."

Did things change? Much to my surprise, my college grades went up, and my stupidities were fewer—fewer, but not all gone. It didn't improve my standing with the "in" crowd, but I didn't care. I was too busy singing and studying. Over twelve months, we probably averaged four or five hundred miles of travel or more per week! Still, I was able to stay in college academically and did quite well in most of my classes, excelling in New Testament Greek, not knowing that I would someday marry a Greek Orthodox Christian. I struggled. But I had found a purpose for living due to the grace of God and the friendship of the quartet.

I think all the guys will admit the quartet was somewhat of an ego trip for us. We sang regularly to all sizes of churches, youth camps, camp meetings, banquets, clubs, TV, radio, conventions, and a few cocktail lounges, reaching crowds of thirty thousand or more. It was uplifting to know that the Arthur Godfrey group and Ed Sullivan's representatives wanted us to audition when we sang at the Miami Beach Convention Center. By this time, we had two new guys at second tenor and baritone, Harrell Lucky and Barth Smith, who took over from Steve Brown. While in Miami Beach walking down South Beach, we were celebrities for a time with a following of groupies. It was heady, and we had our fifteen minutes of fame. We were even invited to do a gig out on Star Island at an unbelievably huge mansion, and we got to select invitees!

Music was my entire life. Many times, I was unbelievably tired after traveling back to the dorm late at night, but it was a good sort of tired. I had a record player next to my bed, and, stacking about eight or ten records on the player (33 rpm), I listened to Glen Miller or the Mantovani Orchestra, hoping I wouldn't need to face the music—an abject fear.

Strange, but after we had those exciting entertainment experiences singing at convention centers to multiplied thousands, big-named hotels like the Fontainebleau and Eden Roc in Miami Beach, the Muehlebach in Kansas City, and to more venues than I can name here, it became routine. I thought I would feel better or, I hoped, more connected to my school, my church, and my friends. From time to time, I still had some of those sinking sand emotions. Would I ever be like other people who had no problems?

Left to right: Danny Steele, Harrell Lucky, Barth Smith, and Marshall Pryor in Miami Beach.

No, we never made it to the big time, but we were a favorite at conventions. Maybe they liked us because they didn't have to pay us as much as the big stars like the Four Freshmen, the Four Lads, the Hi-Lo's, the Platters, and the Ames Brothers. We sang for such notables as the governor of Oklahoma, R. G. LeTourneau (the inventor of large, modern earth-moving machines), and David Ward of Conway, Arkansas, who manufactured yellow school buses sold nationwide, not to mention his friend in Bentonville, Sam Walton.

We stayed in the Ward family home, then went on to the Winthrop Rockefeller estate somewhere close to Petit Jean Park, admiring his Santa Gertrudis cattle. The cows enjoyed it. We were the backup artists for J. T. Adams when his Men of Texas choir was not available. Our first record was recorded in Adams's studio, Towne Hall Records. Capitol Records in Los Angeles did the rest. We gave a concert at the largest Southern Baptist seminary in America (Southwestern Baptist Theological Seminary in Fort Worth) as well as the Texas Baptist Laymen's Convention. We were the lead-in for Shirley Jones (the Partridge Family, the Music Man) at the Dallas Convention Center. Still, the sixteen thousand attendees liked our concert so much, they cheered for thirty minutes, tossing their programs in the air, disrupting the schedule.

We performed concerts in Galveston, Houston, Miami Beach, Dallas, San Antonio, New Orleans, Kansas City, Lincoln, and Omaha. More venues than I can possibly remember welcomed us, including the Delano and Cadillac Hotels; Our Lady of the Assumption Abbey, a Trappist monastery; and Leavenworth Federal Prison. We were singing in over 150 churches per year, and TV and radio station performances over a nine-state area added to our accomplishments. The other three members of the quartet were great guys with incredible talent, and they helped me along.

The fact that the top college music teacher would not accept me as a student because, as he said, I had "ruined my voice," gave me satisfaction. And still, I hurt because of sinking sand.

We recorded two versions of "Memories Are Made of This," a 45 rpm and two 33 rpm albums, one with secular music and the other sacred music. An acquaintance in Carlsbad sent me a thrilling article from the *Carlsbad Current-Argus*. Right on the front page, they lauded our performance at the Dallas Convention Center with the headline, "Ex-Resident's Group Brings Down House."

Ex-Resident's Group Brings Down House

A quartet led by a former Carlsbad youth brought down the house at the Tuesday morning show in Memorial Auditorium at Dallas which was one of the highlights of the Kiwanis International convention, O.H. Smith, president of the Carlsbad Kiwanis Club, reported today.

The group is from Bethany Nazarene College at Bethany, Okla., of which Marshall Pryor serves as master of ceremonies and sings bass.

Pryor is the son of Rev. and Mrs. Luther Pryor of Lake Charles, La. Rev. Pryor was formerly pastor of the First Church of the Nazarene here. Young Pryor's sister is Mrs. Lloyd Davis, 1016 Birch Lane. Young Pryor graduated from Carlsbad High School in 1957 and was a member of the Key Club. Since entering Bethany Nazarene College he has organized a Circle K Club there.

The quartet first sang to 11,000 Kiwanians Tuesday and the delegates stood and applauded so long that Ken Loheed, president, had to rush to the microphone to get the crowed quieted down, Smith said.

After finally getting order, Loheed quipped: "I'll admit they're good, however it's kids like that that knock our convention schedule cockeyed."

Smith said that the Kiwanis program chairman got hundreds of calls following the appearance wanting additional information about the group. He thinks they will get a large offer to turn professional.

The Carlsbad Kiwanis president said the convention was the largest in the history of Kiwanis International with 14,096 registered. That exceeded last year's convention in Chicago by 800, he added.

Merle Tucker of Gallup, which is a member of the Southwest District, was elected vice president. He is former state tourist director under Gov. Ed Mechem.

The article went on and on, stating that we were expected to get a big entertainment contract and turn professional. A great thrill!

We had the privilege to meet and were humbled to sing at a church when the great Christian songwriter Haldor Lillenas was in attendance. He wrote hundreds of sacred hymns, including "Wonderful Peace" in 1914.

We had no way to comprehend what the future held, but we sang at the same youth camp with Bill, Mary Ann, and Danny Gaither when Bill was about twenty years of age. Of course, Bill went on to make his mark in the gospel music business with songs like "He Touched Me," "The King Is Coming," and "Until Then," and the TV program *Precious Memories*.

The Music Stops

My fellow quartet members graduated, and the group disbanded. We loved music and were great friends, but then the song ended. Time to turn over the record. We all stayed close and in touch for many years, and I still consider those guys to be brothers. Time moves on, and Danny passed away not too long ago, and Steve passed away many years ago. I'm one of the fortunate ones—I'm still here, but not all there!

The rest of my graduating class went on to bigger and better things, but I had to remain in college and finish what I had neglected to do as an immature freshman and sophomore. At that point, I didn't have enough credits to earn a degree. I'm not sure anyone can teach a young person how to mature and finish college in four years; it took me four and a half. I was elected second (of course) vice president of the student council and finished college at the end of the first semester. I never made the "in" crowd, and it kinda bothered me at the time, but it was my problem and no one else's. Such is vanity.

During those few short months at the end of my quartet days and before I headed to seminary, I rented an apartment from one of the "saints" of the area. By then, I was newly married to my first wife. With cold weather coming on, my wife and I had to endure the stench of black, sweaty mold two feet up and all along every wall in the apartment.

After I politely asked for a resolution, the landlord asked me, "Why, Marshall Hall"—she was from Texas, so she knew to use my first and middle names as one—"I am so surprised at you. I didn't think you were like that!"

She just didn't "have the money" to handle this problem. It didn't occur to me to press the issue or find another place to live; life was different back then. Maybe that's why I have one black lung and one green one. "Root hog or die," as they say in Texas.

Still, it seemed I deserved every bad thing that could happen, including sinking sand.

9

Seminary

Note to self: Don't make life worse than it already is.

Seminary is that high and holy place newly called pastors-to-be are encouraged to go to lift the collective group up and out of the "cornfield preacher" status. Arriving at seminary was akin to viewing the shining city on a hill. Some called it a *cemetery*, not a seminary, and maybe they had a point.

A little exclusivism was present in the church at large because we were transitioning from the Bible School mentality to a high-class graduate school philosophy. The Kansas City seminary I attended was supposed to be a place of solemnity, a place where the "brothers" were to study theology, the Bible, and how to be a cleric. We didn't wear our collars backward, though. Architecturally, it appeared to be a cathedral and classrooms, all in one great big holy mass of heaven on earth. It wasn't, but I was mesmerized.

The church part was indeed a sanctuary, stained glass windows, pulpit, altar, the whole works. The classrooms were classrooms, but the coffee shop and lounge was a sanctuary in itself. Most of the brothers worked outside jobs and came to class worn out with little sleep. Therefore, the lounge became a place to sit down and take a power nap. I learned to sleep for ten minutes and wake up as though I had been asleep for two hours.

Marital Woes

Men who were ministers, pastors, evangelists, missionaries (or whatever the proper name should be) were supposed to get married, preferably to a woman who could play the piano. Alas, for me, it was not meant to be. At least the piano part.

Barely a few months before showing up at seminary, I was a senior in college with no hint of a wife on the horizon. Then one day, I saw her walk into the student union at college and was immediately struck with her beauty, red shoes, and all. She was a looker. She was about nineteen, and I was twenty-one with the maturity of a twelve-year-old. I thought she would be like my mother, and she thought I would be a real man. Neither were true. We were both too young to fall in love. We didn't. Marriage should never have happened, but it did.

Following three months of "dating," we announced our engagement at the Christmas banquet. She never returned to college.

I'm telling you, I had a vision of learning stuff and pastoring a church. I was hell-bent (sorry 'bout that word) on keeping people out of hell. Here again, with my maturity level so low, someone should have told me the truth: I had no business getting married, no business entering a graduate program, and no business leading others down the path to Christian living when I hadn't been there myself with any degree of understanding. I loved Jesus as much as possible, but a guide can't lead someone on a journey when he's never been there. It's like the blind leading the blind!

"Hold your horses" is what I wish someone had told me. All I knew at the time was singing and focusing on the ministry, as in Colossians 3:23, "And whatsoever ye do, do it heartily, as to the Lord, and not unto men."

Marrying the preceding summer didn't help. I had no idea what marriage should be except hunky-dory. Within walking distance, a few big shots owned properties they rented to seminary students. Some of them were religious slumlords. The slumlords also rented down on Troost Avenue or farther toward downtown Kansas City on The Paseo. Nevertheless, big cheeses competed for the rental income of seminary students.

"Get it while you can!"

That was OK with me. I had other things to think about, especially my deteriorating marriage.

We arrived as po' as Job's turkey. A large, single-family home owned by a church executive was to be vacated due to his move to a huge church on the West Coast. They asked if we would like to rent it at a reduced price, and we were welcomed with open arms. Married life means that it takes two to tango. Newly married, I went along with the tumbleweed, allowing others to make choices for me. Besides, love doesn't hurt when you keep it at arm's length, right? I never understood why, but we rented an apartment in the slums, paying more for rent than we would have paid for the mansion. It turned out to be an enduring metaphor for our marriage.

The hurt in my spiritual heart seemed to seep away into the quicksand of life and time. As St. Paul wrote in Colossians 2:2–4: "That their hearts might be comforted, being knit together in love, and unto all riches of the full assurance of understanding, to the acknowledgement of the mystery of God, and of the Father, and of Christ; in whom are hid all the treasures of wisdom and knowledge. And this I say, lest any man should beguile you with enticing words."

I married a Kansas City girl, and since the seminary was in Kansas City, she and her family were together. All the pieces fit nicely for them. After my mom and dad dropped me off on the college campus along Highway 66, I had minimal contact with my own family. I was moving on. My anchor was to be my new wife, I thought, or wanted it to be.

Both my wife and I were too young, immature, and inexperienced to know who, what, where, and how we should be married. It should never have happened. Her dad and my mother knew instinctively that this was not a marriage made in heaven. But social and church pressure said, "a commitment is a commitment." It was always hell on earth—morning, noon, and night. As fate would have it, we married and moved to Kansas City. The marriage lasted seventeen years.

My Private Hell on Earth

In Kansas City, the winter was harsh, as were a few other things in my life. Ice, snow, freezing rain. Scraping two inches of ice and snow off my 1961 Ford Falcon at 7:00 a.m. and rushing to class on slippery roads at 7:30 a.m. was not a pretty picture, especially after arriving home at my slum-area apartment at midnight and studying until 2:00 a.m.

I was in good physical shape due to years of boxing in high school and playing tennis and lifting weights in college with the quartet guys. It was a good thing, because my schedule was brutal.

My lack of sleep and relentless schedule didn't matter to me. Remember, the Word says in Proverbs 29:18, "Where there is no vision, the people perish." I had a Scripture for everything. I didn't always know what some of those verses meant, but I made out like they were promises, even out of context.

I had grown up, it seems, thinking everything in life was *out there somewhere*. Perhaps it was a coping mechanism. The parsonage was never ours; it was *out there somewhere* because it belonged to the church. Our abodes, the cities in which we lived, and the schools I attended were never permanent; some other exciting place was *out there somewhere*. We were always going to move before long. I never acknowledged my hurts, because that would require me to ask for help. I never admitted my inadequacies, because that would feed my inferiority.

No, I thought. *I'm eating manna and pushing on to the Promised Land!*

I didn't have a Moses on whom I could rely to kill the snakes in the desert. I swallowed hook, line, and sinker a ministerial philosophy of discreet distance. If one becomes too close to a church member, it may show partiality, they said, and I took that to include my spouse. I learned too late that everyone, including pastors, should have at least one meaningful conversation every day. If you can't have one with your spouse, a cankerous, toxic, umbrageous shadow creeps over all relationships.

As it was in college, I was lifted into the heavenlies by the seminary experience. Going to chapel every day was an uplifting adventure that I badly needed, but being tired and worn out took its toll.

Most conversations in daily life are mundane, but not so in seminary classrooms. Discussing the intricacies of hermeneutics, church doctrine, the impeccability of Christ, and the differences between Wesleyan and Calvinistic theology was inspiring. I spent trippy days studying Greek, writing sermons, and sitting at the feet of great intellects and men of faith. Seminary sure wasn't Cisco or Carlsbad. Unfortunately, it wasn't the job of professors to teach me how to mature, but those days at seminary provided me the opportunity to grow up a little and gain badly needed confidence.

Associating with the professors, attending church, listening to the massive pipe organ, and meeting and talking to the biggest names in the international church—man, I couldn't believe it! For the first time in my life, an expansive joy filled my heart. Yes, I was terribly tired, but it didn't matter. God was there, and He helped me mature, learn, and experience spiritual vistas of hope and joy I'd never known before.

I was asked to be the special speaker for many evangelistic services, to sing, and to fill in for area pastors who were on vacation. The Showers of Blessing international radio program director asked me to join their sixteen-voice choir and sing in their quartet. Our radio program was broadcast each week all over the world. They even paid me a few bucks. Then I became the bass singer for a local quartet that, along with the seminary choir, made a record that sold from place to place throughout the church community.

This may not seem so great to others, but to me, I was an active participant in what is written in Hebrews 11:1, "Now faith is the substance of things hoped for, the evidence of things not seen."

My activities not only included many preaching and singing privileges, but classes lasted from 7:30 a.m. through 3:00 p.m., then I was off to a movie production studio where I printed 16 mm movies for a large company making $1.50 per hour (about $11.00 in 2020) from 3:30 p.m. to 11:30 p.m., and then took a thirty-minute drive home where I studied until 2:00 a.m. and was up again at 7:00 a.m. for class. It didn't matter that I fell sound asleep sitting at a signal light on Troost Avenue while people honked their horns and screamed for me to get out of the way.

On weekends, I studied or traveled somewhere to preach or sing. Many times, I took off work at the production company for five or six nights to preach or sing. Fortunately, the company had no problem with this flexibility. Sometimes they required me to come in on Saturdays or holidays to make up the time. Toward the end of my seminary education, I was asked to pastor a small but nice nondenominational country church seventy-five miles north of Kansas City, Missouri. They paid a wonderful salary, far more than I made at the movie production company, and I only had to drive up there on Sundays.

I had finally made it, or so I thought.

All of this was going on while my wife was pregnant and subsequently gave birth to the brightest, smartest, and best-looking son a father could ever have. I had it all!

One Saturday in 1962, I had to make up time at the production company. Some of the seminary brothers and I took a quick lunch at Dixon's Chili café.

Former President Harry Truman liked to dine there. We saw him often but didn't want to bother him. A guy or two was always with him. I guess presidents of the United States like common food, too. At least Harry Truman did. Sometimes he drove up in a big car and other times a plain car like everyone else. While eating, most of the time at least, he was quiet. A few times, he would talk with the men eating with him, but most of the time, he was too busy eating. The chili was good. His favorite. Amazing!

Seminary was a place to research and explore the outer limits of a great theological education designed to lead a church into the heights of spiritual understanding. At a presentation at Calvin Productions, the president of United Artists, a large movie production company, talked to us about what a movie—and by extension, a sermon—should do.

"A movie," he said, "must make people laugh, cry, or sit on the edge of their seat."

From that point on, I determined never to preach in a way that would allow people the opportunity to go to sleep.

A few times, I hit the nail on the head.

Further, from the get-go, I wrote my sermons out in full, preaching from a manuscript without reading word for word. This kept me from preaching about women's hair or lipstick or wandering off on a tangent.

"Marshall Hall"—my dad gave me this advice—"Never major on minors, nor minor on majors."

Toward the end of my time at seminary, a couple of "brothers" from Chicago asked me to meet them at a nearby restaurant. They invited me to join their close group of guys who felt the church needed a strong group of future leaders who would eventually influence the direction of the international church. They wanted to have men who would stick together through thick or thin and promote each other to positions of power. I declined. It seemed like a conspiracy to me. They were shocked and disappointed. From afar, and as the years rolled by, I watched as they indeed promoted each other (there were about ten to fifteen of them)—gaining exposure internationally through conferences, assemblies, and camp meetings and becoming administrators, general superintendents (two), district superintendents (a few), national evangelists, and pastors of the largest denominational churches in the nation. Deep down, I didn't care. I just knew I wasn't on their level. It could have been my insecurities, my plain ol' disgusting independent attitude . . . or maybe sinking sand.

One of my classmates, a so-called lower-level brother who lived with his wife and five kids in the projects, was a part-time pastor of a small church south of the city. He had been a CPA who was called to preach, and he asked me to conduct a series of services from Wednesday through Sunday. I did my best, preaching to about thirty people per service. They were incredibly poor. Like me, he worked for the movie company, and his wife also worked outside the home. Times were tough. I learned that to pay for the expenses of the revival, he and his family prepared rice with one pound of hamburger meat to be eaten over three weeks. I cried. I took no pay.

My wife went ballistic. "We needed that money!"

About a month later, the district conference opened its annual session. Pastors were required to pay a percentage of the gross income of the church to the district and general churches. He had no money to pay anybody anything and none for his family. When it came time for him to stand before the brethren to report, he was unable to confirm budgets paid to the district and general churches. The big cheese in charge humiliated him in front of the five or six hundred attendees. I cried for him and felt his sorrow and humiliation. I got bitter. The church was not as it should be. Sinking sand.

Another disconcerting memory involved the way foreign missions money was handled. Special money raised by local churches for the Thanksgiving and Easter offerings was to be given, as advertised, to foreign missions. Through a closed decision, some of this money was used to pay for headquarters expenses. I understood the need to do so, but I was distressed at the lack of openness and honesty when church leaders still called the monies raised, "foreign missions."

One of the general leaders became so upset by this deception that he led a group of pastors to resign and start their own church denomination. At that point, the leaders decided to call all funds contributed to the general church "world evangelism" instead of "foreign missions." This seemed to clarify the nuance and get them off the hook. It probably did.

Oh well. *What difference, at this point, does it make?* I wondered.

I had begun to sink but didn't realize it. It is amazing how one changes when elected or appointed to a position of leadership. Too often, an attitude akin to bossiness engulfs leaders instead of an attitude that kneels before the needy, washing their feet. Nevertheless, groups tend to elect or support those who use the whip. As in many areas of life, John Milton wrote, "the hungry sheep look up and are not fed."

A multiyear schedule of fewer than four to five hours of sleep per night, traveling here and there, trying to make enough money to support my wife and new son, not taking care of my health, not eating properly, studying, preparing sermons, and singing took its toll. As mentioned, I once fell asleep in my car sitting in heavy traffic at a signal light. On another day, I passed out walking down stairs at the seminary. And another time, while trying to change the oil in my car, I didn't have the strength to unscrew the bolt. My right shoulder was in excruciating pain. It was time to seek help. I didn't have insurance. It didn't matter. I needed help . . . and fast!

The doctor made his thorough examination and said my body was eating itself, and he continued to talk over my head. I just wanted to get going again, but it was not to be.

He said, "Quit or die."

Rather than quit, I made a two-week trip to my parents and hid in a darkened room mostly in a fetal position, despondent and broken. Mother brought soup to the room and, of course, pinto beans with fresh onions, cornbread, and cold sweet milk. I got better.

That's when I knew I had to leave seminary. I grew up in a hurry. The inner hurts and the savaging of my soul was actually a blessing because I matured spiritually. I also grew physically; in fact, I continued to grow taller until about twenty-seven or twenty-eight, which is incredibly rare in the annals of medicine. I am truly a walking, talking medical miracle!

> And He saw that there was no man, and wondered that there
> was no intercessor: therefore His arm brought salvation unto
> him; and His righteousness, it sustained him.
> (Isaiah 59:16 KJV)

The Showers of Blessing choir gave me a wonderful going-away party with gifts, and the brothers gathered around in support. My colleagues, including the seminary and headquarters staff, seemed genuinely sympathetic at our leaving. I was determined to give myself in service come hell (uh-oh, there's that word again) or high water.

Socrates once said, "Know thyself." And Freud said, "Accept thyself." But Jesus said, "Give thyself." By this time in my marriage, I didn't care what my wife thought; I was hell-bent on giving myself to fixing other people. In truth, I was the one who needed fixing!

Sinking again.

10

Pueblo, Colorado

We moved from Kansas City to Colorado, where I took my first job after school. Little did I know that my real education was just beginning. Here is the hard lesson I learned: "Get it in writing."

I abandoned my plan to finish a master of divinity degree program in Kansas City, but I remained committed to becoming a pastor and helping others. It was in my blood. A semi-large church located in a steel town—Pueblo, Colorado—made me an attractive offer to be their assistant pastor, and I jumped at it. They promised a beautiful home and the most substantial salary I had ever made. I took the "job" and moved to where the Colorado Fuel and Iron smokestacks said, "Come on in!"

My troubled marriage desperately needed the stability of a house with a big yard for our child and a white picket fence, but sorry, Charlie! In the sales business, they call it "bait and switch." We were unceremoniously deposited in the Sunday school wing of the church and told to root hog or die. Too late to turn around and go back, so for all practical purposes, we died.

For me, my wife, and our two-year-old son, living there was challenging, to say the least—church kids running, music blaring, fists knocking on our door, and people blasting through the door if we had inadvertently left it unlocked. Late one night, our son started screaming in his little room. I ran in, flipped on the light, and he was standing in his baby bed shrieking. Something black struck me on the side of the head. It flew around, hitting the walls, the ceiling, me, and then my son!

It was a bat!

As luck would have it, the bat flew out the open door into the kitchen and living room. All hell (sorry again) broke loose. Right there in the middle of the night, my wife was ready to move back to Kansas City. I didn't blame her.

The senior pastor, my boss, was a big golfer, so we golfed about four times each week. Because I had no experience, it never occurred to me that he had fallen off the rails. I thought everything he did was what prominent church pastors were supposed to do. I thought everything was excellent! I was in tall cotton. However . . .

Before we arrived in Pueblo, I had no indication the big guy was having an affair with the church secretary. The general church had minimal experience dealing with assistant pastors back in those days since most of our denominational churches had less than one hundred members. They had no need to think through how things would work with additional staff members. Therefore, staff members were expendable and usually blamed and/or fired. He hired me, I found out later, with the express idea of using me as his scapegoat. Nothing personal; I was to be sacrificed for his sins.

One day I received a call from the Colorado DBS asking me to be available for a meeting. He arrived with two other pastors. This naive twenty-four-year-old ushered them to a small room where I animatedly and happily welcomed them. As we sat, the DBS began what could rightly be called an interrogation session. I had no idea what he was talking about. It turned out the pastor had blamed me for splitting the church. I had been there less than four months, for Pete's sake, and was not acquainted with the politics of the people. I was bumfuzzled!

The local congregation's powers that be had picked up on something nefarious going on between the senior pastor and the secretary. The church was in chaos, and I had unwittingly walked into a hornet's nest. Still, the DBS arrived that day to cover his tail by blaming me for the church division. It was ridiculous. After only a few months, I hardly knew anyone in the congregation, much less how I could split them into warring factions.

Around 8:00 p.m., after a six-hour interrogation, some members of the church board heard about the meeting and just about broke the door down and ordered the DBS and his two pastors to leave. Six hours, no food, no water, no bathroom break, just question after question. Well, the die was cast! I started looking for the exits.

My tenure in Colorado lasted barely six months, May to about November 1963, which was just long enough for me to look for and find another job. I needed a real challenge where I believed I could do the most good. So off we went to a tiny church two miles from the Mexican border on a dirt road to live in an adobe parsonage next door to the church. It had to be better, right?

Sinking sand . . . again!

11

El Paso, Texas

By the time I arrived in El Paso, I became a pastor by profession, but in truth, I still had no idea what I was doing. Yes, I could quote Bible verses, and yes, I dedicated my life to God and to helping those less fortunate, but in El Paso, my naivete was stunning.

I did have one thing going for me. I enthusiastically and optimistically embraced each day and knew that whatever else happened, I was determined to be a force for good.

Thank God for Daddy and Mama. We arrived at 9:00 p.m. on Thursday, traveling all day from Pueblo to El Paso, Texas, with everything we owned in a small trailer. Daddy was a master at packing, and Mama helped with our baby son. By this time, my wife was pregnant with our second child. The parsonage was right next door to the church, and things didn't look all that bad—at night.

Early the next morning, I was up and ready to be the pastor of my own church. One of the faithful had left a key in an outside box for us to enter the parsonage and keys to the church. Excitedly, I opened the parsonage door.

The next morning, my dad was already up because it was his custom to get up early, read his Bible, and pray. The two of us entered the church. We stopped dead in our tracks.

"Daddy, what is this?" I asked.

"It looks like they used low-test concrete," he said.

Daddy had extensive experience building churches. In fact, he could make or fix just about anything and knew how to quickly spot and solve problems.

The building was one of those fabricated steel constructions with aluminum and steel beams set on a concrete floor. Unfortunately, the concrete did not have the correct consistency when poured in place. Two-inch cracks spread all through the floor from front to back, sideways, and all around. There were no expansion joints. Furthermore, the concrete had not been sealed, so cement dust was everywhere. The pews had been brought over from a church that closed its doors. Filthy. Out back was a field of weeds native to a desert environment. Well, at least nineteen thousand cars per day passed in front of the church on the dirt road—great exposure!

Since I was young, bright-eyed, and bushy-tailed, nothing deterred me. Nineteen faithful people were there the first Sunday morning, plus my parents. Nine of the attendees were adults. No problem. We had a piano. I played it, sang the special, and preached a sermon entitled, "We Have a Message" from 1 Corinthians 2:1–10.

I preached like a bishop as though a thousand people were there. Daddy and Mama were the only ones who said amen. Oh, and I wore my deep blue, pinstripe suit with a white shirt and red tie, tie tack, and cuff links. No one there told me it was sinful, and it wasn't!

Well, at least I didn't wear lipstick.

My salary was about $30 per week ($800 per month today), plus we could live in the adobe house for free. Not bad, huh?

In the first few months, I mobilized a couple of guys, and we cleaned the place. The only person available to act as a janitor was el numero uno. I still played the piano, sang specials, preached, and visited everybody in that part of town, including Jay, who was a famous private detective who had lost one of his hands to a criminal somewhere. His mansion was on the dirt road; actually, it was more like a zoo. Jay kept monkeys, a tiger or two, an ape, an ostrich, and more.

A water pipe running into the parsonage supplied the kitchen, bathroom, and back porch shower. At first, the shower had a family of scorpions hanging from the top. I politely asked them to move on down the road. With the help of my broom, they complied.

I joined every organization I could find. Soon I was elected to serve as the president of the ministerial association of El Paso, vice president of a local service club, and a member of the Sun Bowl committee bringing football to the city. Man, I was involved! I became close friends with a nearby pastor of a large Methodist church. That was before the Methodist church shifted toward extreme political liberalism and lost members. He mentored me through the maze of my first-time pastorate. Daddy did too, at first, but Mama and Daddy had to go back to Cisco, and my dad was getting old. The more secure Nazarene pastors didn't want to get involved with mentoring because members might leave their church and go somewhere else, maybe to my church on the dirt road.

A few months later, my sweet and wonderful daughter was born. She was so small, maybe five pounds, two ounces. We had no insurance. No money. I didn't have the courage to tell my parents. The doctor and hospital helped because we didn't have any money. She was born with respiratory distress syndrome (I think they called it Hyaline membrane disease) and was at the point of death for nine days. We couldn't touch her, and I nearly despaired. Could my wife take any more of this? She was suffering in an adobe hut on a dirt road with no money and two little kids, stressed out the ying-yang. Sinking!

My time in college and seminary and my little bit of experience didn't matter. I wasn't focused on the inconsequential. I had a church to clean up and a church congregation to build. Our church wasn't the big First Church, for sure. We were known as the low-class church in a poor section of town two miles from Juarez, Mexico. My seminary brothers had moved on to nice parsonages and prestigious churches. It made no difference to me. Just as I had given my time and talent to the quartet in college, I gave it all to build this church, and the church, in turn, gave me some poignant pastoral experiences.

My custom was to study late on Friday and Saturday evenings as a last-minute push toward a sermonic masterpiece. I also used the time and place in my study to think and pray in complete intimacy with

God. I should have known better than to leave my door unlocked. After all, our church was only two miles from the Mexican border and on a dirt road where an amazing array of interesting people were constantly on the move.

All of a sudden, a man flew through the door, blasting it wide open, falling down in front of my desk. I leapt to my feet. He was a new attendee at the church, yelling, crying out, sobbing, blubbering about his failed marriage. He reached in his waistband and pulled out a gun. I was too terrified to run.

Placing his Smith & Wesson .38 on my desk, he cried out, "Pray for me."

So I did. Seminary hadn't prepared me for this.

Before long, a new family moved to our city and attended our little church. Few (if any) megachurches existed in those days. We had to scratch for everything we got. Thank God for the new family. The man was an executive who paid his tithe. The wife and mother had issues; she got all tangled up with a local attorney in an inappropriate way. Her husband, a tower of Christian holiness, asked if I would go with him to confront the attorney. At about twenty-four or twenty-five years of age, what did I know? As any dumb seminarian whippersnapper would do, I accepted.

In Texas, people had guns. We were ushered into a well-appointed office, and the attorney knew why we were there. To send us a message, he opened his top right drawer to show his gun. The godly husband was not confrontational, thank God. Weeping, with a broken heart, he witnessed his faith to the attorney, told him how Jesus had changed his life, and respectfully asked him to change his behavior. All three of us were crying when it was over. The attorney closed the drawer.

Believe it or not, prayer changes things, but isn't it amazing how many of us are tormented by existential questions? These ghastly concerns remind me of a little boy who headed home from my church one day with his family.

He started crying, and his mother asked why.

The little guy said, "The pastor said we should be raised in a Christian home, but I want to stay with you guys."

Like viscous pulp, thoughts of *why* enter our dreams and daytime musings. College and seminary left me completely unprepared to answer life's most important questions.

Does anyone care?

Will anyone attend my funeral?

Will my tomb go unvisited?

Will I ever find happiness?

Is there room for forgiveness?

Will my husband (or wife) shape up and fly right?

Why are we pressured to conform?

Why do some kids have bad parents?

Why do some parents have bad kids?

I prayed, and nothing happened—why?

Why can't I find a husband (or wife)?

Why do I always find the stupid guys to date?

Why do only crazy women want to date me?

Why didn't God make me rich when I sent money to that preacher on TV?

Why do so many find it necessary to point fingers, blame, and judge others?

Am I saved?

Questions, questions, questions!

It's also interesting why and how we dismiss people in our lives. In what hierarchy do we place people? I am dismayed when watching (and experiencing) people being placed at the bottom of the ladder or last on someone's list. Some people are marked valueless, and others are labeled the "in" crowd! If I had written the Ten Commandments, I would have added two more: (11) Thou shalt not be arrogant; (12) Thou shalt not be mean.

All of us have a right to choose our friends and those with whom we wish to associate. On the other hand, can someone have value if they are poor and uneducated? If they have an irritating personality? Crooked teeth? One leg shorter than the other? If they have bad breath? A ripe smell? If they're rich? Jew? Greek? Texan?

Are not all of us God's children?

Perhaps you remember kids in school who placed their fingers in an *L* shape and yelled, "Loser!" When you lose, do you forever forfeit your right to help, hope, and acceptance? When you lose, does that connote no sympathy from us? If someone doesn't measure up to our educational standards or cultural milieu or financial status, should they be called a loser?

One Sunday, a skinny little guy stumbled into the worship service alone, smelling like stale tobacco, wearing shabby clothes. His name was Mr. Weekly, and he said he was looking for work. A few days later, I visited his "home," which was more like a shack. His five kids—twin girls, two younger boys, and a newborn baby girl—were sitting in one larger room with a dirt floor. One of the twins, about eight years of age, was sweeping the dirt floor with weeds she had pulled from outside. They knew I was coming.

The dirt floor was spotless, as was the rest of the house. I invited the family to church. The wife never came, but the rest of the family did, minus the newborn. When they walked through the door of the church the next Sunday morning, the twins and their two little brothers were dressed in their "Sunday-go-to-meeting" best—hair combed and slicked down. They attended Sunday school, their first ever!

Mr. Weekly dutifully went to his Sunday school class and smelled up the place. By then, we were a high-class church because we had a member lady who was a schoolteacher and a guy who was a plumber—and they actually paid their tithes! Oh, and the treasurer and her husband had good jobs, too, but we found out her son was stealing money from her . . . and us!

Some people from a disbanded church visited one Sunday morning. Isn't it amazing how the Holy Spirit works? They entered our "sanctuary" with cracked floors of low-test concrete and an aluminum roof that sounded like a herd of water buffalo running through the living room—no pipe organ, no icons, and no Michelangelo sculptures. We had a piano but no one to play it except me. We had a choir but no one who could sing (four old people and two children).

Despite all of this, God spoke! Some friends from the disbanded church came the next Sunday and brought with them musical talent, friends of Ron Patty, the father of Sandi Patty of recording fame. Most of these new people had attended a Church of God Christian college in Anderson, Indiana. Then, the Sunday after that, some more of their friends joined our family of excited Christians. Soon, neighborhood people came to church. A wealthy businessman and his family were among the group from the disbanded church.

By that time, Mr. Weekly and his kids were regulars. Out of our budget of approximately $7,000 per year, we paid Mr. Weekly $5.00 per week to clean the church. He put his X on the back of his check to cash it. One Sunday morning, as in Acts 2, Mr. Weekly walked to the "mourner's bench"—the altar—to pray, tobacco smell and all. His little twin girls came forward with their daddy and knelt. It was an amazing sight.

Before I knew it, the rich man, wearing his thousand-dollar suit, was kneeling at the altar with his arm around Mr. Weekly. Both prayed and wept as Mr. Weekly gave his heart and life to Jesus Christ. I am compelled to mention that although this happened a long time ago, someone told me that the twin girls went to the same Christian college I attended, and at least one of them married a theology student studying for the ministry. Was Mr. Weekly valueless? Who among us has the right to assign value to another human being?

Do you know what I learned from this? We are all the same at the foot of the cross!

> Though millions have found Him a friend
> And have turned from the sins they have sinned
> The Savior still waits to open the gates
> And welcome a sinner before it's too late.
> There's room at the cross for you
> There's room at the cross for you
> Though millions have come, there's still room for one
> Yes there's room at the cross for you.
> (Ira Stanphill, "Room at the Cross for You," 1946)

As much as possible, the inside of the church was cleaned and fixed up. We purchased a new Hammond organ and an upright piano. At this point, we had a full choir of talented singers and near professionals playing the organ and piano. We had new pews for the people to sit on. We filled in all the cracks on the floor and put new tile down for Mr. Weekly to clean, polish, wax, and gloss. For three years in a row, we were chosen as one of the top ten small churches for growth. We were on a roll.

Small Church Achievement Program

At the annual meeting of the General Board last month, it was announced that the following churches had been chosen as the ten representative churches for 1965 in the Small Church Achievement Program. Congratulations to these churches for outstanding progress.

1. Grove City, Central Ohio,
   Rev. Dale Galloway

2. Phoenix Paradise Valley, Arizona,
   Rev. Dale Horton

3. El Paso Valley, Texas (New Mexico District),
   Rev. Marshall Pryor

4. Spiceland, Indiana (Indianapolis District),
   Rev. William Selvidge

5. Van Buren, North Arkansas,
   Rev. Earl Baker

6. Bishop, California (Los Angeles District),
   Rev. Harry Early

7. Sacramento Cordova, California
   (Sacramento District),   Rev. Bernard F. Colby

8. Colorado Springs Park Hill, Colorado,
   Rev. M. T. Cockman

9. Peterborough, Ontario (Canada Central District),
   Rev. William G. Williams

10. Cle Elum, Washington (Northwest District),
    Rev. Ralph E. Neil

My family life was another matter. My wife was increasingly restless and unhappy with our lives in El Paso, even though we purchased a new parsonage. The church was making great progress; it didn't seem to matter. To me, a major change might make things better, so I resigned, moved my family into a cheap apartment, enrolled in Texas Western College (later to become the University of Texas at El Paso) for graduate studies, and got a job in sales at a large moving company making good money. I kept searching for stability, but every step forward felt like a step and a half backward.

My pastor friend at the Methodist church called. He said, "It is a pitiful shame for you to be out of the ministry! I'm going to call my friend in Dallas and see if he knows what to do."

His friend was the pastor of the twenty-first largest church in worldwide Methodism, with over four thousand people in attendance. The Dallas pastor of Tyler Street Methodist Church told him that he had been looking for an associate pastor for some period of time and couldn't find what he was looking for. He was more of a traditional Methodist with a biblical bent. He said he wanted to call Dr. Robert Goodrich—the pastor of First Methodist Church in downtown Dallas, the largest Methodist church in the Methodist denomination—to get his advice. Why would Methodists want a young Nazarene guy to be their assistant pastor? I presume they talked it over. Tyler Street Methodist sent a committee of people to west Texas to interview me in our jumbled apartment with boxes all over the place.

The committee went back to Dallas and two weeks later offered me a job as the assistant pastor. At first, I was wary due to my experience in Pueblo. Their offer was too good to refuse. Being a Nazarene, I wasn't sure if they were real, honest-to-God Christians, but it looked like a chance worth taking.

As I look back on it now, the silly spiritual flip-flops in my heart and mind were due mostly to my failing marriage. Why in the world did I think leaving the denomination of my birth would signify a loss of salvation? Deep inside, I was in sinking sand . . . again!

12

Dallas, Texas

From the ridiculous to the sublime! I moved my small family from a hovel into a veritable mansion, and I thought it would all go well. Unfortunately, Marshall Hall, the man, was still a work in progress, still trying to figure out how to make other people happy instead of focusing on the greater good. The sinking sand in Dallas was entirely of my own making, as I was unable to solve my marriage issues.

Moving is always unsettling, even in the best of circumstances. The days were filled with anxiety, but our hearts were lifted to the heavens when a real moving truck, Global Van Lines, backed up to our apartment and moved our few worldly possessions to Dallas, paid for by Tyler Street Methodist Church. They even paid for our personal expenses, gasoline, and everything! We had Whataburgers along the way!

I had not seen the home they provided beforehand, so both my wife and I were apprehensive, to say the least. But the grand day arrived, and my parents joined us in Dallas as we gazed upon our new abode. This was not a snout house with the garage sticking out front like a pig's nose. No. As in much of Dallas, the garage was on the back of the house along the concrete alley. This was a four-bedroom brick home in an upper-middle-class area, fireplace and all. We couldn't believe it. In our entire four-year marriage, we had never had the pleasure of such luxury. Yes, we were human with desires like everyone else. We wanted to have nice things. It felt like a miracle.

The people of this large, four-thousand-member church welcomed us with such overpowering friendship and love—no judgment, only warmhearted acceptance. What a beautiful church! I wasn't worthy of this, but I sure opened my heart to it. God's will certainly *seemed* to be in harmony with the increase in our standard of living, and no one would catch me looking a gift horse in the mouth.

These Methodists weren't Nazarenes, that was for sure.

Right from the get-go, I was thrown into challenging but satisfying responsibilities. Two weeks after I arrived, the senior pastor left for South America on a mission and vacation trip, and I was trusted to stand before more than four thousand people and preach while he was away. Oh. My. Goodness! I was accustomed to preaching to about one hundred and fifty people.

My first Sunday preaching went reasonably well, as did the second Sunday. The third Sunday morning was a horse of a different color. I drove up to the huge redbrick church. Twenty-five steps led up into the sanctuary through towering Greek columns like one would see at the Parthenon, and behind them, I noticed smoke coming out of the back of the church. It could have been ol' Brother What's His Name, pastor to the seniors, smoking his cigar, but it wasn't. We called the fire department. The interior of the sanctuary was filled with smoke and fire due to a short in the pipe organ's electrical system. The sanctuary was enormous with its balconies, choir loft, and pipe organ.

Although the greater part of the sanctuary was not in flames, the smoke damage was extensive. The pipe organ was lost entirely, and, I might mention, the new organ cost exceeded $300,000, adjusted for inflation.

We met that morning in the fellowship hall and for months and months thereafter. We added additional services to accommodate the crowd. Our church experienced great growth despite the mishap and forced change of venue.

Despite all the adversity, things went well but, oh, how I struggled with change. I had always been a Nazarene. Jumping ship was way beyond the pale. The elderly associate pastor to seniors was a kindly gentleman, sweet-spirited, courtly, and aristocratic. He smoked a cigar. How could this be?

He was Christian, I finally decided. He just liked cigars instead of Coca-Colas.

When I was about twenty-six, our senior pastor was only thirty-two years old. He never used an outline, book, or any written notes to preach. Amazing! He was a Christian, too. All of the secretaries and staff members, I concluded, were Christians as well. At times, I fought conflict inside my soul, thinking I had backslid, but observing the church people gave me the assurance that God has all kinds of sheep. Still, I decided not to smoke cigars.

A longtime friend and Nazarene college administrator called me and said he would be in Dallas for a district meeting of Nazarene pastors. He wanted me to have lunch with them. I agreed, because after all, I was still a Nazarene. Maybe this would help me keep my roots. Couldn't I be considered a missionary to the Methodists? I walked into the hotel conference room and found a holy coldness among the brethren. It wasn't a holier-than-thou aloofness. They gave off more of a *What Do You Say to a Naked Lady?* air. (Do you remember that show back in the seventies?)

After I was introduced and allowed to say a few words, warmth and brotherhood were restored. Old friendships brought back memories, for I knew most of the guys. I think all of us left joyful and happy. I felt the pull of the Nazarenes to return to the fold, but I explained that I had made a commitment to the Methodists, and I had to honor that. So I did, for a while.

One of my responsibilities was to assist the senior pastor with a heavy load of weddings and funerals, separately. Next door to the main sanctuary (now vacated because of the fire) was a small chapel built for those occasions. It was absolutely gorgeous and seated between one hundred and two hundred people. I was required to memorize the wedding ceremony, and I still know the words to this day. I loved it. I felt like I had finally been pulled from sinking sand, but I was deluding myself.

My experiences meeting some of the greatest pastors of that era still lift memories in my heart—Dr. W. A. Criswell of First Baptist Church of Dallas, the largest Southern Baptist church of that time, and Dr. Robert Goodrich of First Methodist Church, Methodism's largest church. Other great and wonderful pastors, authors, speakers, and leaders were introduced to me as I tried to do my best. Watching and learning from such gifted notables in my field inspired me to improve and grow. Consciously or otherwise, I emulated them in mannerisms, speech, and thought, and I became a much better pastor in the process.

Many people in the Dallas area, including Kiwanians and others, still remembered our college singing group, the Collegiate Quartet. Word got around, and I was asked to sing at various venues. I had to hurry and work hard planning and practicing. I was lucky to have a church member who was a talented musician and could play the organ and piano in any key and any song, so I worked up an entertainment show with jokes and a mishmash of popular songs of the day.

I attended banquets, parties, weddings, and dinners. Being the assistant pastor of a prominent Methodist church was a check mark in my favor, so I was asked to entertain for a large association at the Texas Theatre on West Jefferson in Oak Cliff, not far from our church. (This turned out to be the same theater that Lee Harvey Oswald fled into a couple of years earlier after he murdered President John F. Kennedy.) Performing there was an amazing and thrilling experience for me—entertain on Saturday night and preach on Sunday. Was I supposed to do that?

But I felt the tug from my roots, and each day was a little harder. Nazarene after Nazarene started contacting other Nazarenes, praying I would come back "home." My mama was distraught and hurt that I had left the fold. I said to her that her family, the Parmer clan, were members of the Methodist Episcopal Church South back in the 1800s, so what was so bad about being a Methodist? It didn't matter, she said, because the Methodists had left the holiness camp long ago. But the Methodist book of discipline still listed holiness as a goal to be reached.

I don't know why, but my wife made a trip to El Paso, and while she was there, she met with some people who contacted other people. Then, all of a sudden, the district superintendent (DS) of New Mexico contacted me, asking if I would be interested in moving to Albuquerque. The idea was preposterous.

Here's what I had in Dallas: a beautiful home in an upper-middle-class area, more than an upper-level salary plus benefits, a large church with the prospect of even greater possibilities, and people who were excited to have me there. I held approximately two to three weddings per week and was called on to officiate at funerals regularly. I had a spacious office, no pressure, and was welcomed and accepted by Methodist district leaders and pastors. I was serene and secure. Why would I want to move to Albuquerque to a church on a dirt road with half the salary and live in a small parsonage behind a church that was tiny compared to the Methodist congregation?

I truly never wanted or needed material luxuries, and a rustic life-style suited me fine. No running water? No toilet? No problem. Where could I do the most good? The Methodists in Dallas seemed like they could do OK without me, whereas the people in Albuquerque needed more than a little help.

The factors that weighed most heavily on me, however, were my wife and my parents. Things were not going well for my wife in Dallas, and I believed returning to a small town (or at least a smaller one) might be beneficial for her and our two young children. Moving to Albuquerque would also put me on the right side of things with my parents, and maybe that would tip the balance. It was hard to say. I had a wonderful and great experience in Dallas. I loved the people and I was happy in my job, but still, I decided to submit my resignation.

Was I on sinking sand again? Was I allowing others to bully me again? Did I make a mistake? Was this God speaking or you-know-who? Was I feeling guilty about being a Methodist? What in the Sam Hill was going on?

Okeydokey, there I went again! Same ol', same ol'. Just as it is natural for us to nurture and provide safety for our children, God helps the weak and the stupid. I'm tellin' you—people at the Methodist church were not happy campers with my decision to move.

I blame it on my spiritual genetics, forcing me to pastor little ol' Nazarene churches on dirt roads and go through the pain of being voted on every year to either remain or leave in disgrace. It's some sort of masochism.

And so we packed up our two kids, loaded the car, and left town. No moving van this time.

I regretted my decision the moment we got in the car and were on the road, but it was too late to turn back.

Sinking sand, indeed.

13

Albuquerque, New Mexico

Moving is sometimes a great way to start fresh, wipe the slate clean, and even to slay personal demons of shame, fear, guilt, and despair. But I discovered a problem when I packed up and left Dallas. I brought my personal demons with me.

I left the Methodist church in Dallas under an enormous cloud of embarrassment. Not forced, mind you. Entirely of my own making. Instead of listening to the Holy Spirit, I let other influences guide my decision. We had been in Dallas for a little over eight months.

In a short span of time, I managed to completely lose control of my life. I always got right to the point of success and then made a stupid decision or, more particularly, allowed others to make a decision for me. Did this have anything to do with that horrible day when I was taken advantage of at five or six years old? Reflecting on my ill-conceived decisions always reminded me of the Rio Grande quicksand Daddy and Harold had rescued me from. It was almost as though I was dying—scared and ready to give up.

My low self-esteem infected every aspect of my physical and emotional life. On the surface, however, an unbiased observer might have looked at me and thought I was on the path to great success.

Against all the odds, quite miraculously, I had grown several inches over the past few years. I was now almost five feet, nine inches tall—above-average height. I was strong and in good health, married with two beautiful children, well-educated, passionate about helping others, and yet my life was a wreck. It seemed I was on my road to success by moving to Dallas in the first place. Now, by leaving, I felt as if I was going right back—this time willingly pushed—into the quicksand.

Friends and family thought I had lost it when I took the job with the Methodists in the first place. Now here I was returning to the Nazarenes, sinking down to where I belonged, because I guess I didn't deserve any better. Before Dallas, dirt roads had become normal. Didn't all these people pushing me back realize they were pushing me down? Didn't they know I had preached to and exulted in the applause of hundreds, even thousands? Didn't they know I was driving a new car? Didn't they know past trauma was holding my spiritual legs, crushing me beneath my insecurities, my hurts, my loneliness, and my uncertainties? I was being pressured by others, and my wife, to accept my infirmities, and I was letting them do it! My sinking had to do entirely with my own self-doubt and lack of a clear direction.

Daddy and Mama came again from Cisco with an old trailer. Once again, Daddy helped pack our things. This was becoming a habit. No big truck from Global Van Lines arrived. No money came in the mail to pay for gasoline or Whataburgers.

"God," I cried, pouring out my heart from Psalm 51:12, "Restore unto me the joy of Thy salvation; and uphold me with Thy free spirit."

I hadn't backslid. I got over that stuff. I didn't need to go to the altar every Sunday night. No, I was just confused by change, marriage, money, and children who needed me. Yes, I think I had grown accustomed to my "poor me" attitude.

Was I hungry? No, I was *starving* for hope. I was heading for the desert, and my tongue was parched with abject loneliness. And yes, I know God watches over little children and sometimes the stupid. I didn't feel it, but the great God of heaven was preparing a river of living water that flowed from deep within. There was a fountain, like in Psalm 46:4. Old Belial, that worthless serpent, that deceiver, told me my own immaturities and stupidities caused all of this disruption, and things would never change. Satan accused and abused me as I drove across the barren land of western Texas and eastern New Mexico with the old trailer hot on my tail, piled high with our junk. One would think a bunch of dust-bowl Okies was heading west to Bakersfield. Deep, deep down in my heart of hearts, something changed. I had always been one to excel when pushed against the wall. God was there. I didn't fully realize it, but sure as shootin', He was there.

We finally arrived in Albuquerque. Yep. Dirt road. Just my style. Teeny, tiny lil ol' parsonage. At first, I heard Belial say, "This is what you deserve."

But then that Someone, the Rock, spoke. "I brought you here for a purpose."

"OK," I replied. "I'll accept that. Show me what it is."

"Why don't you just take this assignment one step at a time and quit telling me what to do? It's about time you left your little pity party. I've got it all planned out, so quit whining. Just do your job."

Does God talk like that? Well, He did this time! All of a sudden, that Scripture came to mind from Jeremiah 33:3, "Call unto me, and I [. . .] will show thee great and mighty things." Did God put it there? Was it an epiphany? Or was it just wishful thinking? Was I trying to force-feed my starving soul? Nope, not this time. I heard it! Clear as day.

Was I beginning to find out what being on solid rock was all about? The Solid Rock was not prestige, power, being liked, nice things, or money. In the grand scheme of things, we have absolutely no substitute for the Solid Rock.

My hope is built on nothing less
Than Jesus's blood and righteousness
I dare not trust the sweetest frame
But wholly lean on Jesus's name.
(Edward Mote, "My Hope is Built on Nothing Less," 1834)

My predecessor was a guy who totally focused on building the church and looked to the next generation, young people, as the center-piece of his ministry. I think he had three sons who were good kids, and they started bringing friends from school. Before long, they had forty or fifty teenagers in the church. I followed him at just the right time. God's timing!

The church property was badly in need of repair and an upgrade. Mobilizing the congregation to accomplish this was easy because they could see the fruit of their labor. Rather than lick my wounds after the embarrassment of leaving Dallas, I jumped in and worked hard to clean up things around the church. Coinciding with this was my desire to use this marvelous group of young people. Being only about ten years older than the teens in the church, I took a survey of the talents they possessed. Many, if not most, could sing. Some could play instruments. A few of the church adults were musicians as well.

When I laid out a vision of a teen choir, it caught fire. We started with approximately thirty kids in the choir and four or five adults playing guitars, horns, piano, and organ. We chose a few songs, and off we went into the wild blue yonder. The congregation was amazed and thrilled. This teenage choir became our launching pad for growth, and soon we had approximately forty kids with some adult musicians, helpers, and sponsors.

The former pastor built the congregation from almost nothing to a gathering of wonderfully unified people who were ready to push through the gate like racehorses at the Kentucky Derby. Although they had built a small classroom area just prior to our coming, the property needed help. While the church got larger and larger, we steadily made improvements.

We were in Albuquerque for more than three years. During that time, I grew physically, spiritually, mentally, and emotionally. My hard work was beginning to pay off in many ways, and I started feeling stable. My parents were getting older and were living in Cisco on their own. My daddy retired seven years earlier, and my mama spent most of her time looking after him. Wouldn't it be great if we could all be together again? A little house next to the church became available, and I persuaded my parents to move in. The day before they were to move from Cisco, my dad passed away. He was seventy years old, way too young to die.

The news and the timing of his passing left me stunned. Why

would God take him from me the moment I needed him the most? I was on the Rock, I thought, but it felt like sinking sand. I was looking forward to my daddy's assistance. It had been almost ten years since I had spent an extended period of time with him, and I realized how important he was to me.

Now he was gone.

When will this ever end?

I got knocked around all the time. I was under the impression that things were supposed to get easier as I grew in grace and the knowledge of my Lord and Savior, Jesus Christ. I was convinced I could ask anything in Jesus's name and *presto*, a genie would pop up before me and say, "What would you like, sir?" Was I this nuts after being reared in the church, going to a Christian college, attending seminary, and experiencing everything I had?

When anyone follows in the footsteps of Jesus, Satan—the accuser, the deceiver, the liar, and the adversary who transforms himself into an angel of light—will be there to create chaos in any and all ways—guaranteed. Sometimes you don't feel like you are following in Christ's footsteps. Your feelings deceive you, as did mine. When you are going through the desert of hard times, you may not have air conditioning, but as 2 Corinthians 4:17 says, your "light affliction, which is but for a moment, worketh for us a far more exceeding and eternal weight of glory." As described in Hebrews 11:25–26, Moses chose "rather to suffer affliction with the people of God, than to enjoy the pleasures of sin for a season" and esteemed "the reproach of Christ greater riches than the treasures in Egypt." Acting this way will require you to surrender to the One who promised in Deuteronomy 31:6 to "not fail thee, nor forsake thee." That's called faith!

After my dad's funeral, I threw myself into work with a new intensity. Members pooled their funds and purchased a school bus, which we painted blue and white. Others put a luggage rack on top. We had a vision! The choir, The Melody Makers, was really getting good. With youthful vigor, I directed them, prayed, preached, and had the time of my life. These kids were not only good, they were excitedly Christian. We were ready to go on the road.

We mapped out something like a twenty-five-hundred-mile trip to various churches through Texas and sang at the original Astrodome in Houston. I think this may have been the highlight of most of our lives at that point. Was this an experience of crass enthusiasm or God's guidance? I chose to think God had His hand in it. What if I had stayed in Dallas? I don't know.

It may be in the valley,
Where countless dangers hide;
It may be in the sunshine
That I, in peace, abide;
But this one thing I know—
If it be dark or fair,
If Jesus is with me,
I'll go anywhere!
(C. Austin Miles, "If Jesus Goes with Me," 1908)

I needed to lay aside those hurts of childhood, stupidities of high school and college, and memories of the past. As Philippians 3:13–14 advises, it was time for me to forget "those things which are behind," reach "forth unto those things which are before," and "press toward the mark for the prize of the high calling of God in Christ Jesus." God hadn't taken away my immaturities, stupidities, insecurities, inferiorities, or mistakes . . . yet!

God helps those who help themselves, and so, of course, He hadn't removed that "thing" in my nose, either. Of course, He wanted me to get off my seat and do it myself. So I called Dr. Sadok, who agreed to restructure my nose at no charge. I made an appointment at the hospital. While in the operating room, the nurse gave me a shot, and suddenly, I couldn't move a muscle. I had no feeling, but I knew what was going on. I felt the pressure of the doctor cutting the base of my nose, peeling back the skin, and murmuring to his surgical nurse.

Buzz. He sawed the bone in my nose.

Then he said, "Hit it here."

The nurse took the hammer and hit my nose. After a few more buzzes, pushes, and hits with the hammer, I went to sleep. A day later, I awoke with cotton ropes up both nostrils, sick as a horse. The next day, Dr. Sadok came in and pulled something like fifteen feet of bloody rope out of my face while a member of the church, Lottie Houts, watched and provided comfort. I could never again use that "thing" in my nose as an excuse for my inferiorities. All along, God was working on my character through my pain and uncertainty.

The church grew—packed out—more than I can possibly recall. Let it be said that out of that church came over thirty, maybe thirty-five, young people who were called by God into Christian service, some to missionary work, others in pastoral ministry, and some as spouses of the clergy. Many others are serving to this day as faithful lay members of their local church.

After steady growth over approximately three years at the Albuquerque church, it was time to move on. Yes, despite all the success my church was having, my marriage and family life were crumbling.

On a Sunday afternoon, after preaching to a packed sanctuary, my marriage erupted in controversy. Bawling like a wounded cow, I drove to the DS's home, pouring out my tormented heart to the DS and his wife. The hurt was more than I could take. Maybe another move would help the situation.

It didn't.

I packed the trailer myself. Daddy and Mother were not there to help. I was really sinking this time.

Time Traveler

More than forty years later, in 2011, a friend of mine and I decided to go on a "bucket list" trip to visit places we had lived throughout our life. Driving into Albuquerque going east on I-40 in my little Mercedes SLK 320, I was shaken by the barrenness of the New Mexico desert. It still had a certain charm with the Sandia Mountains looming over the valley and the tram lifting high up to ten thousand feet. Turning off the freeway onto Wyoming Boulevard, I noticed I no longer knew my way around. I knew where Central Street was, so I found my way to Moon Street. I drove by the old parsonage behind the church and turned the corner onto Erbbe Street. The road was now paved but otherwise mostly unchanged. And then

I remembered a horrible day, a day when my world almost came crashing down.

On the corner of the church's road, where my precious children had been playing shortly after we moved to Albuquerque—on dirt streets, of course—an out-of-control car wheeled off Central onto the dirt street, making a complete circle and churning up a cloud of dust. Gunning, it made another furious circle in the dirt. A cloud of dirt boiled up exactly where my children were playing, and for ten heartbeats, all I could see was a thick, angry cloud, believing I had lost both of my children under the car as it lurched to a stop.

Screaming and crying, I ran toward the murderous scene. All the while, Apollyon, Satan the destroyer, ridiculed me.

Finding my precious ones unharmed, I rushed to the car where three men sat. Grabbing the door, I yanked it open and noticed all three men were catatonic. I didn't care how big they were or if they had a gun. I was willing to gouge, hit, bite, and kick to defend my children, pastor or no pastor.

Then I noticed some strange instruments on the steering wheel. The young man behind the wheel began to cry. He had no legs. His car was built especially for him. Through his sobs, he said that the instruments had stuck, and he couldn't get them loose to stop, so he turned off on the dirt road, hoping he wouldn't run into anyone on busy Central Avenue. I was ashamed, not knowing what to do.

Deep in my heart, God spoke.

In my 2011 visit, seeing where I had left my blood, sweat, and tears almost took my breath away. Up high on the tower constructed while I was there, the front part of the church and the back of the sanctuary, was the 650-pound bell that Mama had in her backyard in Cisco, a bell Daddy had as a keepsake. A member of the church and I had hoisted it up on a trailer and pulled it all the way from Cisco, Texas. There it stood high on the tower, and no one would ever know the story behind the bell or how it got there. I cried.

14

Sacramento, California

Being a pastor gave me the privilege of meeting hundreds of people from all walks of life every year. Quite often, I met them on the best and worst days of their lives—joyous wedding ceremonies and gut-wrenching funerals. Watching their highs and lows gave me a lens for my own experience and made me appreciate the gift of life all the more. Though I sank lower into the sand, I knew bedrock was some-where down deep. Moving to Sacramento forced me to plumb the depths of the Holy Spirit.

I had no idea where we were going, which was also a metaphor for my life. I was asked to pastor a church in the North Highlands of Sacramento, California, a rather blue-collar area. I had no GPS to rely on in 1970, and the map wasn't complete. After I called a number sent to me, I was told to go to a certain inexpensive motel along Auburn Boulevard and register. The church had no money. The year before our arrival, the church's gross income was reported as $19,000. More than three hundred people regularly attended, but 79 percent were children under high school age. We stayed in the motel for three weeks and visited the church for the first time on Friday, June 19, 1970.

At long last, we were allowed to drive to the parsonage, which turned out to be the beginning of our trek through our own Sinai

Desert. The place was spic-and-span, but it certainly wasn't like the new parsonage in Albuquerque and for sure not like Dallas. It was in a lower-income area. That was all right—my style. The street was paved, not dirt. Whoopee! I was already waist-deep in the quicksand of life—marriage—although God was teaching me about the Rock.

But grow in the grace and knowledge of our Lord and Savior
Jesus Christ. To Him be glory both now and forever! Amen.
(2 Peter 3:18 NIV)

Pulling into the parking area of the church, bypassing a vacant lot of star thistles, I entered the church that could seat about two hundred people and walked to the pastor's study. Welcoming me was a floor of rat droppings—that's it. No desk, no chair. Guess who showed up to welcome me with a big ol' smile? Right. You guessed it.

The destroyer said, "You're a loser!"

Satan is an evil angel cast out of heaven. His express purpose is to defeat and destroy God's good plan in our life. I presume the destroyer mitigated things by having a lady show up with a chef's apron on—mustard and catsup included—to welcome us. Nice lady.

My wife went nuts (in private to me, of course).

I wasn't overly enthused, but I had been to far worse places before. Living in squalor didn't bother me.

Don't get me wrong. Not everything was bad, negative, and wrong. I was a go-getter and had a vision. Maybe I should have spent more time at home. Things were worse at home than at any church. I was struggling against sinking sand long before I married, but let me tell you something: trying to lift people up while fighting at home was not easy.

In Carlsbad, on July 4, 1956, one month before I turned eighteen, I knew with absolute certainty that Christ the Savior entered my life. There was no doubt about it. My life changed; however, being reared in a pastor's home, along with extreme immaturity, seemed to gloss over deep spiritual understanding. My faith was more of a cultural thing. I knew all the concepts, but implementing them in my life was quite another issue.

Why did I choose the ministry?

I didn't. It chose me!

My wounded heart, the sinking sand syndrome—a vacant shove—seemed to be saying I was just the one who could fix people who needed fixing. I did not have the maturity nor the desire to be a psychiatrist or a forensic psychotherapist. I had the desire to be like Daddy, a pastor. My fragile emotions mimicked the performance of an inept knife juggler, sometimes catching the knives by the handle, and sometimes slicing my hands without obvious pain. My spiritual life was more like mumbo jumbo—sincere, prayer, loving, and wanting to be of service to everyone in need. However, I just flat couldn't get it together.

In the old days when pastors and priests were respected as the chief cooks and bottle washers, I preached, prayed, sang, directed congregational singing, sometimes played the piano, cleaned, pulled weeds, and painted. More importantly, troubled souls would come to me for comfort and counseling. Since I didn't know what to do or say, I usually remained quiet and listened. It seemed to work, because most people just wanted someone to listen to them.

For whatever reason, the vibe in my Sacramento congregation started badly and quickly worsened. Maybe Californians responded poorly to my Texas accent, or maybe my mannerisms were too different. It's hard to know. Instead of radiating magnetism, I seemed to bring about repulsion.

My first day on the job in North Highlands was June 21, 1970, and I preached the same sermon I preached in El Paso, "We Have a Message."

And so it was with me, brothers and sisters. When I came to you, I did not come with eloquence or human wisdom as I proclaimed to you the testimony about God. [. . .] However, as it is written: "What no eye has seen, what no ear has heard, and what no human mind has conceived"—the things God has prepared for those who love Him—these are the things God has revealed to us by His Spirit.

(1 Corinthians 2:1 and 9–10 NIV)

A good man, a solid leader of the church, took me aside after my first sermon in North Highlands and advised me, "Pastor, if you continue to preach like that, you will have problems in this church."

I found out later that his warning came as a compliment. Indeed, the passage of God's original calling for me to preach, 2 Timothy 4:3, made the warning clear: "For the time will come when they will not endure sound doctrine."

I had virtually no contact with other pastors at the time and no concept of California culture. Believe me, California was and is different than Texas and Oklahoma. Back in the day, the congregation voted each year to determine whether a pastor should stay or go, and their word was final. Each church had its own calendar, which was always a mystery to me. During the five months before my election, I noticed money was missing from the offering plate. When I appointed a committee of three faithful men to investigate the deficit, hell broke loose. They found the culprit, who turned out to be an usher and counter and wore a big ring of keys. He and other relatives of his were not happy campers, but I dealt with him, although I never exposed him publicly or in private conversations with parishioners.

In the end, after he was removed, I solved the problem by changing the money-counting process, but some members of the congregation didn't think I had done anything. In the election, I squeaked by with one vote above the required 50 percent. Hallelujah, I could stay for another year! Five families stood up and left the church with all their kids, right there and then. That same morning, I preached like a bishop and made an altar call so people could be born again. No one got saved. They were too worn out from voting, and so was I.

Maybe we oughta have a church split, I thought, so we could create some new Christians. Whoopee!

My life might have gone better if I had lost that election. Sometimes we get what we pray for and then wish God hadn't been so responsive.

I went back to the grindstone, just like in El Paso and Albuquerque, pulling weeds (star thistles), cleaning stuff, moving into and organizing a pastor's study, knocking on doors, and preaching and praying and trying to hold my family together.

In the days that followed, the church experienced explosive

growth. But in any group, some people want to impede growth, consolidate their power and influence, and impose their will on the masses. Human nature. Unfortunately, I had a survival instinct in me akin to bullheadedness. Sometimes good and sometimes bad. Nevertheless, I was able to marshal (no pun intended) enough people who went door-to-door and invited people all over the place to church. Then we started a singles class in a motel along Auburn Boulevard—for Bible study, of course. It grew like crazy. Soon, excitement took hold, and attendance doubled.

More importantly, the presence of the Holy Spirit moved with power and grace. Lives were changed. Families were reunited, though not my own. "Heaven came down," and glory filled our soul, or so the song goes. Soon we had two services on Sunday morning, then three, then another baptismal service in the afternoon and two on Sunday evening, one of which was a teen service. We went from a tiny parish that was hardly making it to one of the most successful and fastest-growing Nazarene churches in the country.

We hired associates and musicians and purchased a seventeen-acre property. The church brought in architects and faithful laymen who knew what they were doing. Out of nothing but raw land, I saw the vision of a church that would spring from the ground, and in my mind, it was beautiful—at least the first phase.

I had no doubt about it—the Holy Spirit of God through Jesus Christ was there. Despite the outward appearance of success, I felt like a failure.

A uniqueness hung in the atmosphere of the church services like the beginning of the early church in Acts 2 when the Holy Spirit indwelt the followers of Jesus. As commanded by the risen Christ in Acts 1:4–5, the 120 disciples were required to "wait for the promise of the Father," for "ye shall be baptized with the Holy Ghost not many days hence." We believed it! We experienced it! It had nothing to do with a new church building. It had to do with obedience.

The true Holy Spirit indwells us when we offer our human heart to God after repentance. Like oil and water, He goes to the place of least resistance. Jesus was a human being, having been sent as God in the flesh, the Son of God! When Jesus voluntarily died for our sins, arose from the grave, and ascended back to heaven, He gave those who hungered to be pure and holy the Comforter, the Holy Spirit. The Holy Spirit becomes a guide to our spirit, an enabler. John 16:13 clarifies, "When He, the Spirit of truth, is come, He will guide you into all truth." In John 14:26, Jesus says, "But the Comforter, which is the Holy Ghost, whom the Father will send in my name, He shall teach you all things."

I didn't completely understand the fullness of it all, but the Spirit of God took the lead.

The old saying is "inch by inch, it's a cinch." Therefore, He took the lead. He was our *Comforter*! He was the One who led us, surrounded us, loved us, and became the "little red light" in our soul. He, the Holy One, gave us the inner understanding of purity. He is the One who told us the difference between good and evil. As long as we walked in His light, His glory, the joy of the Lord was our companion! Was I not walking in His light by building a new church to His glory? If so, why wasn't His light shining brightly in my own home? Miracles took place in the church community! Why not my home? *Solid Rock,* I thought, but it wasn't.

Anything that cuts your heart to pieces, I learned, anything that destroys your peace, anything that produces hopelessness, anything that deletes that still small voice of God in your soul is a demonic spirit. Multiplied thousands of spiritually evil, demonic creatures are looking for an opening. The evil one will come to you as an angel of light, making you think good is evil and evil is good.

When Satan fought to keep the church from being built, God made a way. Even when the community architectural committee (headed by a guy from another denomination out of Salt Lake City) turned us down for the design of our new building, God made a way. When our church district advisory board made us stop construction—probably due to jealousy—God was there. When a woman marched up and down the street with a big sign protesting our theology, God intervened. God was even there when a drug addict stripped his clothes off during our early Sunday morning service, ran down the aisle to the pulpit, strangled me, and pulled a baby from her mother's arms, all with blood and foam running from his nose and mouth. God used it all for His glory. Over the next few years, hundreds were converted, making a definite commitment to Christ. The first phase of the new church building was completed.

Missionary Zeal

In 1972, I introduced something called "Faith Promise" to the church. Few churches at the time had heard of the foreign missions plan of Faith Promise. Instead of giving money for missionary programs only at Thanksgiving and Easter, we encouraged people to step out in faith and give to others throughout the year. The church was growing in numbers and giving; therefore, they financed a trip for my wife and me to the islands of Trinidad and Tobago. I was to preach to the island churches, missionaries, and teachers. It was the experience of a lifetime, a chance to absorb a new culture while spreading the Word of God.

One evening in the jungle, I preached to a small group of spiritually hungry aboriginal Christians in a thatched-roof church—about seventy-five indigenous people and another thirty or so missionaries and their families. Toward the end of my sermon, an enraged young man, the son of a missionary, jumped up and rushed toward me, angrily yelling.

The muscular young man screamed at me as he hurled his fist at my face. I was shocked—actually stunned—and had no time to protect myself. I watched as his huge fist was propelled with lightning speed toward my face.

Shockingly, it didn't matter. His fighter's fist miraculously disappeared. How could this happen? He followed through again. It was as though an unseen, supernatural being of some sort (perhaps an angel of God) made his fist disappear into nothingness.

Immediately, his dad jumped from his seat to pull his son away. The angry young man spun and with a clenched fist hit his father so hard that blood splattered all over those nearby. For over twenty minutes they fought, knocking chairs over, wrestling as though they were MMA fighters. People cried as the huge men fought, the father trying to protect himself and others from his deranged son.

I urgently invited people to pray. The blessed Holy Spirit was there. So was an evil, demonic spirit! Missionaries regularly tell of strange, evil spirits working against the Christian faith, some going through an exorcism. Those are the same unclean spirits spoken of in Matthew 8:28 and Mark 5:1–20.

Be careful, my friend. You cannot violate the Holy Spirit!

> Be sober, be vigilant; because your adversary the devil, as a
> roaring lion, walketh about, seeking whom he may devour.
> (1 Peter 5:8 KJV)

After that experience in Trinidad in 1972, when I returned, I noticed a spiritual movement taking place in North Highlands. Lives were changed, like in the story Dr. J. Sidlow Baxter wrote in his devotional *Awake My Heart*.

An Anglican priest happened to be looking through his parsonage window when he saw a workman enter the church. The man returned at the same time every day, twelve thirty in the afternoon. The priest was curious, so he sent a spy to wait for the man before twelve thirty.

The man entered, stuffed his cap into his jacket pocket, and walked down the main aisle, to the rail in front of the communion table. There, with bowed head, he stood in silence. Then, putting his hands on the communion rail, and looking over toward the communion table, he said in a low voice, "Jesus . . . it's Jim."

A terrible accident occurred days later at the construction job where Jim was working, and a number of men were injured. Jim was one of them. He was taken to the hospital and placed in the ICU. After a few days, he was taken to a ward where some of the other construction workers had been admitted. The men had been rough and crude with their language and disrespectful to nurses. After Jim had been there two or three days, the sisters noticed a marked change. The room had settled down amazingly.

One morning, just as the sister entered to start her round of the beds, the men were all enjoying a good-natured laugh at something. She could not help asking the first man what it was which had made such a change in them all.

He replied, "Oh, it's that chap in the fifth bed. They call 'im Jim."

So when the screen was round Jim's bed, she said to him, "Jim, you've made a wonderful change in this ward. Tell me how you've done it."

With a tear glistening in his eyes, Jim replied, "Well, sister, I'm not sure you'd understand if I told you. But somehow, every day, just about twelve thirty, I see Jesus at the end o' my bed. He stands there for a minute, then He just puts His hands on the bed rail, an' leans over, an' says, "Jim . . . it's Jesus."

Yes, the Holy Spirit, the Rock, was with the church and me.
I soon learned a hard lesson, however. When hurts and afflictions

arise, when one is hit in the nose of life with problems, it does not mean that the Rock has forsaken you.

> For our light affliction, which is but for a moment, worketh for
> us a far more exceeding and eternal weight of glory.
> (2 Corinthians 4:17 KJV)

The next few weeks would test my faith and ultimately strengthen it, but first I had to endure the most difficult period of my life, making all my previous near-death experiences seem like a cakewalk.

15

Divorce, Disgrace, and Destitution

For a Nazarene preacher in the 1960s and 1970s, no greater shame existed than divorce. How could a congregation look to a preacher for moral and spiritual support when he could not hold his own family together? The idea of divorce was anathema and completely out of the question, but after years watching the foundations of my marriage crumble, they finally broke. With my marriage went my career and my purpose, but blessedly not my precious children. Were it not for the presence of God, we would have been alone and destitute.

Unfortunately, Satan struck again—at the heart of my family. From the beginning, my marriage was not to be. Due to a combination of my immaturity, poor decision-making, the cross-purposes of culture, change, and from my viewpoint, betrayal of what the ministry should be, my marriage fell apart.

I felt no need to take someone else's knife and stab myself with it. I was reared in a home that taught, "Others, Lord, yes, others, let this my motto be." Everywhere we moved, I was trying to pull myself out of sinking sand. In the end, in Sacramento, my wife left our two children and me. We had nowhere else to go; it felt like certain death.

The destroyer is tricky. He is the same spirit that worked on the mind of Eve, making good seem bad and bad seem good. An evil spirit will make you scared with sad, anxious, or angry feelings while at the same time dominating your emotions with excitement. Whispering, the evil one speaks like he did in Genesis 3:5, "Go ahead. Eat this fruit. You'll become just like God!"

Vaunting itself as a frolicking angel of fun, he captures your desires, giving you the sense you are something special. Satan does it all the time, dressing up as a beautiful angel of light. Even priests, pastors, pastors' wives, professors, politicians, and others can be sucked in, taking advantage of the vulnerable.

"Give me your money, and you'll be healthy, wealthy, and wise. Give me your body, because God is love, isn't He?"

Satan's servants disguise themselves as servants of God, as 2 Corinthians 11:15 says, but they'll be paid in due time for their deceit.

I knew how to maneuver in the sand, but I had no idea what to do with a broken marriage. No one, not even the great God of Calvary, chose to teach an emotionally immature kid how to heal his hurts. I was so busy healing everyone else's hurts, I couldn't attend to my own family. An old preacher put it this way: "You are too busy building a bigger orchestra to tune the instruments, and so involved in chopping wood, you don't have time to sharpen the ax."

It's entirely human to hurt and to ask, "Why?" Down deep in my soul somewhere, the evil one spoke. I have no words to describe the laceration Satan imposed on my soul. I could almost hear the demons of hell laughing, taunting me, making fun. A poison was injected into the veins of my heart. Perhaps you have been there.

In my darkest days, I took solace in the words of Jesus from John 16:33, "These things I have spoken unto you, that in me ye might have peace. In the world ye shall have tribulation: but be of good cheer; I have overcome the world." I found comfort in reading my Bible, especially Psalm 56:4, "In God I will praise His word, in God I have put my trust; I will not fear what flesh can do unto me."

No one understands like Jesus;
He's a friend beyond compare.
Meet Him at the throne of mercy;
He is waiting for you there.

No one understands like Jesus
When the days are dark and grim.
No one is so near, so dear as Jesus;
Cast your every care on Him.
(John W. Peterson, "No One Understands Like Jesus," 1952)

The pain and torture in my mind were beyond anything I had ever known, but in that moment, I finally understood that my suffering had meaning. I could not just give up. What would become of my two young children? For their sake, not mine, I had to find a way to keep going. The Christ of Calvary pulled me out of the spiritual and emotional sands of life, but for what purpose? I came to understand He wanted me to learn more fully about the Solid Rock!

The first few days after my wife left, I tried to make myself believe life would return to normal. I was a pastor, and I had a temporary place to live, even though the house belonged to the church. Of course, the future would look much like the past, except now it would be my two children and me instead of the four of us. I would keep going. I might decide to move to another church, because moving cleaned the slate, right?

But God had other plans for me!

The phone rang. I ran into the kitchen and grabbed it off the wall, perhaps thinking it would be someone offering me a job I hadn't applied for.

"Hello."

A loud voice, spoken with a staccato cadence, commanded my attention. It was the DBS. I was a trustee of the regional university and a board member of the district financial institution (credit union). Furthermore, a few pastors had asked me to help them with a series of services. It didn't matter. I hardly knew my name anymore. Most pastors, however, had never faced this situation before. A leading pastor going through a divorce? That was not supposed to happen.

"Do. You. Think. I'm. Crazy? You act like you are purposely defying leadership *and* the Manual," he bellowed.

Bumfuzzled, I said, "Well, I'm not quite sure I know what you mean."

"You have no reason to stay on! You know what the Manual says about divorce!" I was served with divorce papers just two days before. How did he know?

Truth be told, I didn't know what the Manual said. Actually, at this point, I didn't care.

Once again, Belial spoke hastily and laughingly said, "Quickly, tell him that the Manual also says you can't share a pool with both women and men or go to the theater either."

Isn't it amazing how penetrating Satan can be? Having been bullied most of my life, I got my hackles up.

Confused, I said to the DBS, "Are you asking for my resignation to both the financial board and the college board?" Those were the only two positions I had retained.

I had the phone to my left ear because I'm left-handed, even though I'm hard of hearing in that ear. He shouted back at me. "You need to resign from *all* of your positions."

"Brother DBS, if I'm not mistaken, the Manual also says that you are my 'administrative' leader, not my boss . . ."

I didn't realize it, but the phone was dead. Apparently, he had hung up.

From that point on, a raised eyebrow from the DBS or a click of the tongue or a dark smile told the brethren that I had leprosy. Acting quite unlike Christ, I kept my positions for one more year. I had nothing to hide! And I held a few services to boot. Wasn't that awful of me?

Speaking derisively to the DBS worked on what little conscience I had left, but I realized that despite all my good work, my success in building the congregation, and my devotion to the church, I was not welcome. Little by little, I was pushed aside. So I finally mustered my courage and resolved to bring the situation to a head. I called the DBS's office and made an appointment. I also called a few ministerial friends (I had one or two left) and asked for their prayers, since I was going to see the big cheese.

The big day arrived. I was equipped with a nice suit and prayer following my tail. I opened the door to the office and noticed a certain cold and sour look on the secretary's face. Without saying a word, she stood up and walked hurriedly to a back room where I surmised the DBS's office was located. Even with my bad ear, I heard her say, "He's here."

My steps clipped on cheap tile to his office. With folded arms and red face, he sat, looking at me, not saying a word.

I broke the silence. "I just wanted to come by and ask your forgiveness for speaking disrespectfully . . ."

Before I could continue, he barked loudly enough for people in the apartment building next door to hear. "Do. You. Think. I'm. Crazy?"

I had already heard this! The meeting was over. With that, I walked out—and never returned.

No more sand, but . . . where was the Rock?

I found out much later that one of the brethren had spread a rumor in the district ministerial meeting that he (or his wife) had heard that someone had said (or told one of his or his wife's friends) that I had run off with a woman and was in Hawaii . . . he thought!

Reeeally? As they say in Texas, "Hep us 'n' bless us."

They didn't know I had visited my sister on her dime with my two children at the La Brea Tar Pits in Los Angeles. Oh well, people gossiped about Jesus, too.

"Isn't this the carpenter's son?" [. . .] And they took offense at
Him. But Jesus said to them, "A prophet is not without honor
except in his own town and in his own home."
(Matthew 13:55–57 NIV)

Money meant little to me. Who cared? God takes care of His own— my parents taught me that. As a pastor, I lived paycheck to paycheck and had no savings. What little I had in the bank went to my wife when she left because she had no means of support. The kids and I moved out of the parsonage, and I began the fruitless search for a place—any place—to live. No money. No home. Nothing!

In two weeks, my children and I would be homeless. I swallowed my pride and asked my mom for a few bucks, but she had no money. She had lived the life as a pastor's wife and was seventy years of age.

A funny thing happened on the way to Tinseltown, that is, Hollywood, California. I saw a sign that said, "For Rent." The owner met me at the rental apartment, and I asked if he would negotiate the rent, and he said *no*. He said the rent was as it was to keep the riffraff out. I could certainly understand, but as I left with my tail between my legs, I felt the sinking sand moving up to my armpits.

No job, bumfuzzled, no one to turn to, hurt beyond measure! I had lost control. Sure 'nuff, the old accuser Belial made his presence known. He always showed up right when I really didn't want the hassle.

"See, I've told you all along you shouldn't have moved to California. You were not mature enough to lead a growing church. Building that church was a mess, and you knew it all along. The advisory board turned you down because your members were too poor and low-class to build a big church building, and furthermore, you shouldn't have started building it with cash. Remember, it sat there for nine months. Seventeen beautiful acres with only the foundation finished—nothing else. Didn't you know you had no experience building things? What an idiot. Besides, where's your God?"

I said out loud, "Look, I don't want to hear this. I've got enough problems as it is. God is right where He has always been." The Rock, through faith!

"Really, now," Belial mocked. "You better wise up, 'cause He isn't anywhere I can see. Do *you* see Him? Be honest. Has He ever talked to you, or is it a figment of your imagination? Have you ever seen an angel? Remember when you were in Louisiana, praying? You thought it was to the 'Almighty,' and you thought you saw Him? Well, you didn't. Come on. For the first time in your life, be brutally honest with me . . . and yourself! You're on the outside now. Hey, man, you're free! You don't have to fake it till you make it anymore."

My career as a pastor was over, and I knew it. That big red letter *D* would be forever tattooed on my forehead. In those days, the church bureaucracy had a tendency to shoot our wounded. Oh, I know, some carried on—the overcomers. I wasn't strong enough. Too weak or prideful. I had been bullied all my life, and I wasn't gonna take it anymore. I was the one who was supposed to show kindness and empathy, not the other way around. My pride wouldn't allow me to let people know I was financially upside down.

It hurt, but at least it didn't feel like sinking sand. For the first time in my adult life, I was an ordained pastor without a church, but at that moment, I rediscovered my relationship with God.

That night, I had a dream. I walked to the front of a little stucco house. It had a big picture-frame window. All the brethren were inside, talking and laughing and holding their drinks, cocktail-party style. I'm a-gonna promise you it wasn't wine or anything unacceptable to drink. I found no doorbell—in my dream—since this was one of those houses built in the forties or fifties. I knocked, and the DBS opened the door. When he saw me, he shut the door. I turned and walked away, and as I looked back, one of the brethren pulled the shade down over the picture-frame window.

The dream was over. At this point, I didn't know if I was in the sand or happily running down the yellow brick road.

Unemployment Line

I wasn't dirty. I just dressed down so it would look like I needed some help from the "gubmint" unemployment benefit office. Even $100 would help. Jumping into my big, brown 1976 Thunderbird with less than one-quarter of a tank of gas, I left the house thinking I would walk right in and present my case. Confident all the way to Watt Avenue near I-80, I was puzzled when I saw not a huge office building but a warehouse with a thousand cars parked outside. I parked away from the other cars so no one would bang their door into the side of my car and walked hurriedly to where people were standing in a line halfway down the sidewalk. I was confused. This didn't make sense. Didn't these people know I was a pastor (or had been until a few days earlier)? Not to worry. I would go inside and talk to the nice lady and walk out with my $100.

Hello? Is anyone in there?

After I was unceremoniously ushered back out to the end of the line, which had grown by ten to fifteen lost souls, I inched my way forward over the next two-and-a-half hours. In the meantime, babies were screaming, kids were running everywhere, smoke was billowing, and loudspeakers were blaring. The stench was horrible. Not one person there knelt and called me blessed! No one kissed my ring because I didn't have one to kiss. Finally, finally, I was called to a window with a hole in it. The "lady" sitting behind the window took a full thirty seconds to look up at me. So I waited! And waited!

(*Stop!* Wait a full thirty seconds before you read again, and see how long thirty seconds is and imagine standing that long in front of the powers that be!)

Then she lazily looked up. "Yes. May I help you?"

(Well, at least she said *yes*—a positive word.) She did not say, "Well, hello, pastor!"

With a ministerial voice, hoping no one could hear me, I said, "I'm here to apply for unemployment."

Irritated, she groaned. "What is your Social Security number?"

That sounded hopeful. I was well on my way to getting my $100, which would help feed my kids. Not enough for rent, but at least they wouldn't be without food. Computers were not as efficient in 1977 as they are now. She waited, and waited, and waited—and so did I.

"Who was your last employer?"

With my ministerial voice, I whispered quietly.

Didn't she know I was the pastor of a growing, up-and-coming church? Didn't she know we had purchased seventeen acres of land and dedicated the first building project three weeks ago?

Apparently not!

Suddenly, the crash came! In a monotone, she said, "You can't collect unemployment. Your employer didn't pay anything in. Next!"

I stood there in stunned silence, trying to take in the meaning of her words.

"Next!" She waved me away.

Back in those ancient days, pastors were considered self-employed independent contractors for tax purposes, which meant the church did not consider me an employee for purposes of withholding. In fact, I was never a church employee and never received a W-2—only a 1099-MISC. Of course, even if I had known the difference, I wouldn't have cared. My important work as a pastor superseded the federal government in every respect.

Except now I understood all too clearly that neither my church nor my country would take care of me. Walking away from the unemployment window empty-handed was a shattering experience.

I was broken . . . spiritually devastated and financially crushed, rock bottom. Was this sinking sand again? Where was God? I was out of the sand and on the Rock, knowing that in this world, I would face tribulation. But things like this were not supposed to happen to people like me.

Why God? Why?

As I sobbed on my way to Bertha (my big, brown 1976 Thunderbird), Belial whispered in my ear, "Do you remember that sermon you preached about the meaning of my name, calling me 'worthless?' Well, that is exactly what you are. You're not worth squat! You've lost it all. You've never really been a success at anything you've ever done. You have always gravitated to all those little, low-class churches on dirt roads while all your college and seminary friends became big shots. Furthermore, none of your people had money. Just think about it—do you remember pastoring that little church two miles from Juarez, Mexico? Didn't you hear me when I told you not to move to El Paso? And what was the first thing you saw in your 'luxury' office when you moved from Albuquerque to Sacramento?"

"I already know."

"Well, what was it? Tell me!"

"Rat droppings."

"See? That's exactly what I'm trying to get across to you. You're not worth anything. You have no money, two children who need food, oh, and let me ask you—who do you think will hire you? You don't know anything about anything. Businesspeople don't hire preachers!" Mockingly, he added, "What're you gonna do, preach to customers?"

While he was laughing, I jumped into the car and drove home, crying my eyes out. Arriving, I fell on the ugly, gold-colored shag carpet in abject spiritual and emotional poverty. I screamed imprecations on my wretched life! I had two kids who needed food. I had no money. We had only two more weeks until the end of the month, and then we would be homeless.

And then I remembered a hymn, and I sang the words to myself. It gave me the strength to get up off the floor, dry my eyes, dust myself off, and get to work.

> O soul, are you weary and troubled?
> No light in the darkness you see?
> There's light for a look at the Savior,
> And life more abundant and free!
> Turn your eyes upon Jesus,
> Look full in His wonderful face,
> And the things of earth will grow strangely dim
> In the light of His glory and grace.
> (Helen Howarth Lemmel, "Turn Your Eyes Upon Jesus," 1922)

I finally sank so low, all the way down through the sinking sand, and what did I discover? Miraculously, I was standing on Solid Rock.

16

From Sand to Solid Rock

My identity was tied up in the notion that I was a pastor. Surely I earned the respect of others because I devoted my life to God, right? When I left the church and gave up that identity, I realized my chosen occupation was vanity and God did not care whether I led a congregation or dug holes for a living. What mattered was doing right by my fellow man and helping others in need. For that, theological training was helpful but not required. Once I accepted the idea that I could spread the word of Jesus through my actions and that I did not need to look toward an institution to hire me as an independent contractor, I could slay my inner demons and stand, for once, on Solid Rock.

The sign in the window said, "Help Wanted," so I stopped and applied. It didn't matter what kind of work it was. For the sake of my two children, I needed a job—any job.

The more you need a loan, the less likely a banker will be to approve it. The same principle holds true for job seekers. The more you need to find work, the less likely an employer will be to hire you. I had lost all confidence in myself, and people could smell my desperation a mile away. I had no skills in applying for a job, so I went everywhere and applied for everything.

I had heard of a Catholic priest who left the priesthood and married some gal in the Sierra Mountains. He was driving a logging truck. *Great, I'll do that!* I quickly learned I would need to get a special license by going to a school—blah, blah, blah. No go.

A 7-Eleven store came into view. The Middle Eastern guys behind the counter heard my accent and laughed me out of the store. I applied to a messenger company, a hotel, and a thousand other places. I interviewed to be the associate pastor at another local church of another denomination. No help. No hope.

In desperation, I walked to a bank in downtown Sacramento. The manager of the bank had given the church a loan a few years before. He was a nice guy, so I asked to meet with him, and fortunately, he was available.

I said, "Art, thank you for making time for me. I'm not sure if you have heard, but I am no longer the pastor of the church. My wife chose to move on."

"What's that got to do with cheese in China? Maybe you're lucky," he said. Then he laughed. I wasn't quite sure what he meant.

Tears came into my eyes. At that point, I couldn't stop crying. Can you believe it? Why would I be crying in a bank? How embarrassing.

The next day, he called, asking me to meet him the following Wednesday at the Sutter Club, a dignified, elegant business club downtown, to meet a client of his. Why? The guy, his client, might have some work for me. It didn't sound hopeful, but I wasn't going to say no to anyone who might hire me. After all, I was close to homelessness.

I showed up wearing my Sunday-go-to-meeting pinstripe suit. Art's client was wearing a cheap suit, blue polyester, and black shoes with mud on them. I had no idea what business he was in or that he was one of the wealthiest men in the United States.

It wasn't until much later that I learned he was the largest contributor in the State of California to the Democratic Party, and he owned seventy-eight skilled nursing homes plus real estate, forestland, shopping centers, a golf course, and investments in about everything. We talked and basically shot the bull. Nice guy. A little peculiar.

At the end of our lunch, I was given no job offer and not even a "let's keep in touch." He said, "Good to meet you." We shook hands and went our separate ways. I later learned he had his investigators check me out through some of my church members. Days went by, during which time I applied for several other jobs, and my lunch meeting was a short memory. Then on a Saturday, a week later and early in the morning, the phone rang.

"Hello."

"I'll pick you up in thirty minutes." He hung up. I guess he knew I would recognize his voice.

To myself, I said, "What does he want? Why is he coming here? Are we going to a restaurant? How am I to dress?" Hurriedly, I shaved and threw on the only other suit I owned with a red tie. I dressed in an inexpensive sport coat with light brown pants. My shoes were the same ones I wore when I applied to a neighboring church as assistant pastor and was sneered at as the two guys interviewing me happened to see the $28.00 price tag sticking to the bottom of my shoe. I was ready and waiting. If I had known what was to come, I would have dressed like a Philadelphia lawyer.

His limousine pulled to the curb. *What door should I use?* I opened the back door. He was there.

He said, "Sit up front."

I put my tail between my legs and sat with the driver.

During the drive to downtown Sacramento, I thought he wanted me to be his limousine driver. I would have taken the job. Anything to keep my kids off the street. Then I thought, "He already has a driver!" I put my mind in neutral.

The driver pulled to the curb on Capitol Mall, and my employer-to-be (Let's call him "The Man" henceforth!) courteously asked me to follow him. We walked to the elevator in a tall building and rode up to one of the top floors that opened into a spacious law office.

Is he a lawyer? A businessman who will give me a job?

The Man had barely said two words to me. We were immediately invited to the inner office of a crude old lawyer. I was not introduced. The two of them—my "future" employer, The Man, and the lawyer—engaged in rapid conversation. The lawyer boorishly used filthy language; he had been drinking. It was about 8:30 a.m.!

Who drinks at eight thirty in the morning?

They were talking about politics and money-sharing information

146

far above my pay grade. In my confused mind, I thought, "Why is he allowing me to hear this confidential conversation?" I was just a guy sitting there, not knowing who, what, when, or where.

When they finished their talk, we left. I presumed The Man knew I would follow him downstairs. We walked down ten or fifteen floors to the first floor. I was huffing and puffing by the time we reached the first floor. I later found out that The Man ate apples and steamed vegetables, exercised, and was as strong as a bull. The driver was outside.

The Man was interesting, to say the least. He was a good person, but different. First, I didn't know why he called me. Second, who was this guy? Third, he sure didn't look like someone I wanted to be associated with. Fourth, he never gave me the impression he wanted to hire me or, if so, what to do or what my salary would be. He wasn't rude; he was simply peculiar.

We got back in his limo—I sat up front—and drove all the way to San Francisco, about a ninety-minute ride. He never said one word to me. Pulling up to the City Center, we exited the limo and walked to the mayor's office, occupied by George Moscone. (The following year, George was assassinated.) I was introduced, but that's about all. George didn't kiss my ring, nor did he bow down and call me blessed (he must've been Catholic, or maybe I was just too dadgum prideful). Having spent two hours with him, George propped his legs on top of his desk, laughing, joking, and talking about politics and people. The Man didn't laugh.

After their conversation, The Man and I walked across the street to a greasy spoon café, and both of us had soup. It's a good thing he paid for it, because I didn't have a dime. Later, the limo drove us to the Getty mansion overlooking the Golden Gate Bridge for a cocktail party. Yes, Getty, *that* Getty—Gordon and Ann. I was completely out of my league.

The Man (my employer without a portfolio) didn't drink alcohol. I didn't either. The Governor of California, Jerry Brown, was there. George Moscone, Dianne Feinstein, and a mix of celebrities and print notables were there also. I was there in my cheap suit. It didn't matter, because The Man and a few newspaper people didn't look high-class.

Making a deal with Governor Jerry Brown.

*Marshall Pryor (far left) with Jerry Brown (center) and Senator
McCarthy (back turned on right) at the St. Francis Hotel.*

Marshall Pryor with Joan Baez at the Getty mansion.

After the Getty cocktail party, as many attendees as wanted to walked a few doors down the street to the Shapiro mansion. We were to be introduced to a new, young, up-and-coming politician (this was 1977). Standing in the entryway of the home, the young politician arrived to give a short speech. (It wasn't short, and the gaggle of mouthy women there were not impressed.) It was a thirty-five-year-old Senator Joe Biden and his brother, Jim. I had no idea who this Biden was, nor did I care. After they left, we followed.

The Man and I were driven to the Fairmont Hotel to spend time with Joe and Jim. We sat in the cocktail lounge, the four of us, as Joe and his brother drank. Neither The Man nor I had alcohol. They talked about things I didn't understand or care about. My mind was on my kids, my lack of money, and the fact I had no idea why I was there. I couldn't understand what I had been thrown into.

I took it for granted that I was employed, not knowing what my job description was. I was told to be at the office on Monday morning (I had to borrow money to buy gasoline to drive to his office). I don't recall ever receiving or accepting a formal job offer, but the following week, I started receiving paychecks and learned from The Man's in-house attorney that I was to be the executive assistant to The Man.

Senator Allan Cranston and Marshall Pryor (left).

*Lt. Governor of California Mervyn Dymally (second from left), his
wife Alice (third from right), Marshall Pryor (second from right),
and other guests on either side.*

All the time I spent in those luxurious surroundings made me feel
guilty, thinking of my kids. Thank God for some wonderful members
of the church who lived nearby. They were marvelous, loving, and
beautiful people. All I had to do was call them, and they would watch

over and, in some instances, take my children to their home for a day when I had to work. They were "heart friends," lovingly supporting our family in that awful time of distress.

I wished so much that I could have worked from home, spending more time with my children during this time of transition. My heart ached—and still does! My mother flew to Sacramento shortly after my employment and provided comfort and help, as did my sister. No substitute on earth exists for the love of family and friends who care enough to give their best. I am reminded of the song we sang in those little churches of my childhood:

> There's not an hour that He is not near us.
> No, not one! No, not one.
> No night so dark but His love can cheer us.
> No, not one! No, not one!
> Jesus knows all about our struggles;
> He will guide till the day is done.
> There's not a friend like the lowly Jesus,
> No, not one! No, not one!
> (Johnson Oatman Jr., "No, Not One," 1895)

A Clean Break

Through work and diligence, I got back on my feet. I was no longer financially destitute, no longer facing the threat of eviction and home-lessness. I made more money than I had made in my entire life. My children and I did normal things like going to the zoo and getting burgers at McDonald's, and my kids attended the same church I had pastored. One evening, I received a call from my successor at the church—late at night. It woke me up, in fact!

In that dignified voice that all pastors are wont to have, clearing his throat, he said, "Brother Pryor, I think it would be more fitting for your children to attend another church. Now don't get me wrong; they are wonderful young people, but a clean break might be more appropriate."

He must have been getting advice from upper management. Was I truly hearing what I was hearing? Never in my life had I ever heard of a pastor turning someone away from their church. It was unthinkable, uncharitable, and unchristian. I didn't sleep for the rest of the night.

The early morning time was spent in that netherworld between heaven and hell. If purgatory exists, I was in it!

Once again, Belial whispered in my ear. In my mind, his name changed to Beelzebub, the dung god. He said, "You ain't worth squat!"

I wrestled the rest of the night between intense anger, shock, heart-aching agony, and worthlessness. Neither my successor nor the DBS could point to a single thing that would justify such a petty, insecure request. As a result, I realized people are always going to act like people.

Satan needles, but God pinpoints. Everyone has their own horse to ride. So what? Where was the Rock? When all else failed, I read God's advice to Joshua after Moses died.

> Be strong and very courageous. Be careful to obey all the law
> my servant Moses gave you; do not turn from it to the right or
> to the left, that you may be successful wherever you go.
> (Joshua 1:7 NIV)

If I placed in writing my two years spent traveling the world with my employer, The Man, meeting with the movers and shakers of business, government, finance, and Hollywood, attending lunches and dinners exceeding $25,000 per plate ($100,000 in 2020), you would either be stupefied or skeptical. No, the money was not for rubber "chikin." Most of the money went for political donations . . . and, of course, influence. At this point, another book could be written detailing those experiences—without names to protect the innocent.

After two years of this, I resigned from my position rubbing shoulders with mayors, governors, representatives, senators, Hollywood celebrities, the monied, and the nouveau riche. It wasn't worth it. I was tired of sitting at tables with people who only knew how to babble with no depth, people with shadows but no substance, people who could only talk about other people, people pretending to pretend they were not pretending.

I was indeed grateful for the opportunity and the nobility of doing honorable work, but I didn't see how being a rich man's executive assistant was benefiting anyone but him and me. However, that time working for The Man gave me insight into the way the world worked and the confidence to believe I could some day build my own business. I also learned a hugely important lesson from The Man that stayed with me even to this day.

"If you don't know something—ask," he would say.

There is no shame in asking any question, no matter how basic.

A friend who owned an educational business was probably singing the hymn, "Rescue the Perishing" when he hired me to be the business manager of his growing empire of schools (real estate schools with seventeen different locations and bank training, escrow training, and contractor testing schools). He had been a neighboring pastor and was the owner of his own businesses. He laid it all out and turned it over to me. A few years later, he was elected to pastor a large, prestigious church and was there for about twenty-nine years. I licked my wounds and carried on. No regrets. Later, I became a business and tax consultant, a stockbroker (Series 7), a Life Underwriter Training Council Fellow (LUTCF) in insurance, a financial planner, an owner of various business operations, a real estate broker, a land developer, a builder of custom homes, an owner of a Hawaii business named Snuba, and, finally, an owner of assisted living facilities.

Challenging? Yes. Always successful? No. Thrilling? Absolutely!

In the grand scheme of things, it matters not if you are a US Senator in a wrinkled suit; a strong governor of the eighth largest economy in the world; a silly mayor of a large city; a big church pastor, little church pastor, or not a pastor; a butcher, baker, or candlestick maker; or a big shot, little shot, or no shot. "Where Jesus Is, Tis Heaven" there.

Once heaven seemed a far-off place,
Till Jesus showed His smiling face.
Now it's begun within my soul;
T'will last while endless ages roll.
What matters where on earth we dwell?
On mountaintop, or in the dell?

In cottage or a mansion fair,
Where Jesus is, tis heaven there.
(Charles J. Butler, "Where Jesus Is, Tis Heaven," 1898)

Free at Last

It recently dawned on me—I am above the age at which many of my older friends have passed along. They didn't worry about things, and so neither do I. Age has found its home deep in my breast. I had grab bars installed in the shower, LED lights placed in strategic locations because the elderly (a classification I proudly fit in) needed more light. I don't trust myself to climb ladders anymore (real or metaphorical). Tomorrow I have an appointment with hospital staff to walk me through their clinic, since I'm now beginning to forget things. Later on, the doctors will test my hearing . . . and I have been told I have the early stages of Parkinson's. More and more, I'm careful about spicy foods.

Other than when I invited Christ into my heart and the birth of my two wonderful children, meeting my wonderful wife, Carole, about forty-one years ago was the most beautiful and wonderful event of my life.

I was sitting in my office, looking out the window. Coming up the stairs was a lovely young woman, a kindergarten teacher. How did I know? She wanted to receive her real estate license during the summer months. I knew because I was the business manager. Her face told me she was sweet-spirited.

Abraham Lincoln once received a recommendation to hire a person for his cabinet, but he refused. He was asked why.

Lincoln replied, "He doesn't have a good face." He meant it physically and metaphorically.

Carole had—and has—a sweet face, a loving face, a beautiful face! Across these forty years, she has proven to be the sweetest and most loving person I could ever possibly have as a companion. She has helped me grow in maturity, intellectually and spiritually. A life of joy. How could I ever . . . she is a rock.

Carole and I married in a Greek Orthodox wedding on June 21,

1980. The wedding was marvelous, although it scared me, making the transition from Nazarene to Orthodoxy! The next day, we were driven to San Francisco, took an Eastern airlines flight to Atlanta, Miami, and then spent our first night in San Juan, Puerto Rico, where we stayed in Old Town at the Hotel El Convento. Two days later, we flew to Point Pleasant in St. Thomas and stayed six days. There, we laughed, swam, dined, and had the privilege of attending a Commodores venue to hear Lionel Richie and "Once, Twice, Three Times a Lady." From there, we went to Martinique.

After spending a few days in Martinique, we were to fly to Mexico City. However, Eastern airlines was going bankrupt, I think. We went to the ticket counter in Martinique, and the agent did not want to speak English, only French. Carole stepped up and started speaking to him in French. That sealed it! He put us in first class on Mexicana airlines, where we had first-class treatment, steak and all. We flew to Guadalupe, where we spent more time, then back to Puerto Rico and on to Mexico City for a few more days. We traveled to the pyramids outside Mexico City and visited the Palacio de Bellas Artes and Chapultepec Castle, where the French Emperor Maximilian I and Empress Carlota resided back in the 1800s. America beckoned us to New Orleans for a few days and we made our way back to Sacramento through Dallas and San Francisco. We were gone for twenty-one days.

Carole and I have had wonderful times going places, experiencing the joy of life, jumping in the car or flying somewhere, not knowing where. One time we took off for Dallas to see some of our kids and grandkids, rented a car, and toured thirteen southeastern states. Driving through the bayous of south Louisiana, we noticed we were lost. We pulled off the road to a small place with a sign that said, "Information." We went in and asked for a map. The attendant said she didn't have a map, but a fishing shack on a gravel road may have one. We received directions to the shack, jumped back into the car, and took off. Two young women were standing out in front of the shack.

I lowered my window and asked, "Do you have a map?"

One of the girls spoke up and said, "We don't got no map, 'cause we know where we at."

Carole and I laughed like crazy for an hour as we found our way back to civilization.

A trip through eight western states came the next year—Las Vegas and all the national parks of Utah, up through Idaho and Wyoming to Yellowstone, on to South Dakota and Mount Rushmore, then Colorado, New Mexico, and Arizona. And of course, our place in Puerto Vallarta, Mexico, always beckoned us.

On our twenty-fifth anniversary, we were in Kowloon atop the Peninsula Hotel in the evening, looking across the harbor to Hong Kong Island before our dinner arrived. We watched as hologram lights danced through the skyscrapers. Both of us cried, remembering how God had blessed us. At the same time, we both took a deep breath of thanksgiving.

A different book could be written about our experiences over the last forty-one years, but for a different purpose, namely to express our deep gratification in the presence of God and remembering how He loves us and blessed us. His presence is far more important to us than anything we have experienced in this life. Carole and I have traveled from Greece to China, Europe to Central America (where we watched howler monkeys jump through the trees and crocodiles swim along-side our canoe), Alaska and throughout the continental United States (from Washington, DC, to Seattle, Washington), Japan and Korea—hither and yon, here and there. Nevertheless, the best times we have had are when we pray together, relishing the glory of His presence. Carole has been a sweet, loving, beautiful Christian wife and companion beyond my wildest dreams.

We are at peace, standing on the Solid Rock. I pray I can bring others to stand there alongside me, too.

In the Presence of Real Kings

Carole and I were sitting with my son, his wife, and our grand-daughter outside, having dinner at a restaurant in Carmel, California. A motorcycle CHP officer rode up and parked. I laughed to myself, thinking I would go tell him this was not a Dunkin' Donuts. Then two more drove up—I was outnumbered.

A rather old-looking Suburban parked right behind the motorcycles.

Doesn't that guy know what he's doing?

Then two nicer-looking Suburbans parked behind the old one. For about five minutes, nothing happened. Then a few guys exited the cars while the motorcycle cops milled around. We continued to eat.

Our server came to our table. We asked what in the world was going on. She didn't know. That's the state we're in most of the time. "We know nuttin'!"

Then a short guy opened the door of the old Suburban, walked back to the new one, opened the door, and entered. He remained in the new one for about a minute, exited the far side, and as a few big guys surrounded him, he walked within six feet of us and entered the restaurant.

It was the *king of Jordan*, Abdullah II! Whoa! He seemed like a regular guy.

We continued to eat. It was interesting, but not life changing. Then I remembered that on July 4, 1956, the King of Kings and Lord of Lords walked by my heart. Determinedly and passionately, I followed the Savior to the altar. He showed me His heart, hands, feet, and side. He said through Matthew 11:28–29, "Come unto me, [. . .] and I will give you rest. Take my yoke upon you, and learn of me; for I am meek and lowly in heart: and ye shall find rest unto your souls."

I confessed. I surrendered and said,

> Just as I am, without one plea,
> But that Thy blood was shed for me,
> And that Thou bidst me come to Thee,
> O Lamb of God, I come, I come.
> (Charlotte Elliott, "Just As I Am, Without One Plea," 1835)

When the King of Kings and the Lord of Lords passed by my heart, my life changed.

> Could my tears forever flow,
> Could my zeal no languor know,

These for sin could not atone;
Thou must save, and Thou alone.
In my hand no price I bring,
Simply to Thy cross I cling.
(Augustus M. Toplady, "Rock of Ages," 1775)

Continuing On . . .

Now, as Carole and I look out over the eighteenth green from the nineteenth hole at the Carmel Country Club with the Pacific Ocean breeze wafting across my face, enchanting waves are kissing the shore, humming a soothing lullaby of eternity, stirring long lost hurts, anger, insecurities, inferiorities, and sins—memories! All of those noxious and pernicious negativities of my childhood and acidic experiences of life are barely visible through the fog of time. As described in Micah 7:19, they've been cast into the sea of God's forgetfulness. Sinking sand is no more. The Solid Rock is forever!

Lone Cypress at Seventeen-Mile Drive, Pebble Beach, California, USA. Photo by Alexey Potov. CC BY 2.5. No changes made to original photo.

We visited one of the most photographed trees in the world, the Lone Cypress, that has been subjected to fires and the storms of the

Pacific and grew out of hard granite rock. It is reportedly 250 years old and has suffered much over the centuries. Even today, held up by cables, and through its pain, it continues to bring joy to millions who see it every year. It was even featured on TV during the Pebble Beach Pro-Am golf tournament. Few give a second thought to what that Monterey cypress had to endure to grow there.

At this point in my life, sinking sand, hurts, gossip, and the disappointments of life mean little. Few understand the winds of life, the crashing waves, the hard granite, and the hurt that brought me to this place. No exuberant urgency moves me to achieve. No fervent excitement. No dancing through the tulips. No fluttering around trying to be accepted. Just as Daddy and Harold rescued me out of the quicksand in the Rio Grande River, I have had the marvelous privilege of associating with amazing people of all kinds who have added color, intellectual stimulation, and growth to my life. Many have brought hope and help. Others have lifted me with love.

Most of us have benefited from people who have enhanced and lifted us to new heights of joy and love, having a significant influence on our life. Often they are teachers, pastors, and neighbors. A few of those influences have had a powerful impact, enough to change us. But only One has given us life more abundantly. Only One has the power to transform us. He is the Solid Rock! At last, the spiritual hurt in my heart has seeped away into the quicksand of time and maturity. Thanks to Jesus, I have inner peace.

> Coming to Jesus, my Savior, I found
> Wonderful peace, wonderful peace;
> Storms in their fury may rage all around,
> I have peace, sweet peace.
> (Haldor Lillenas, "Wonderful Peace," 1914)

Daddy resigned this church of life on February 17, 1968, and Mama, as she had always done, followed him on December 21, 1991. They both reside in that parsonage in the sky; it no longer belongs to someone else. It's not on a dirt road. It's on a street of gold. They own it. Jesus, the Son of the living God, paid for it and handed it over to them free of all restrictions and debt—no mortgage. He lives there, too.

> Let not your heart be troubled: ye believe in God, believe also in me. In my Father's house are many mansions: if it were not so, I would have told you. I go to prepare a place for you. And if I go and prepare a place for you, I will come again, and receive you unto myself; that where I am, there ye may be also.
> (John 14:1–3 KJV)

I'm going there, and Carole will be with me. Jesus said we could own our own parsonage. It's not on a dirt road; it has gold just like Mama and Daddy's. I won't be required to pay a down payment. The purchase was made with blood. It's built on the Solid Rock! He built it. He promised it. I believe Him! And . . .

> When the toils of life are over,
> And we lay our armor down,
> And we bid farewell to earth with all its cares,
> We shall meet and greet our loved ones,
> And our Christ we then shall crown,
> In the new Jerusalem.
> (C. B. Widmeyer, "When the Toils of Life Are Over," 1911)

PART II

FAITH ANSWERS

17

My Story

This book is a testament to my faith. Through my stories, I hope others will learn salvation is through faith, but having faith alone will not immunize you against bad things. Surely my own life proves that point.

You have questions, as all of us do, but I do not have all the answers. What I do have, however, is unwavering faith and a lifetime of trying to help others in need. May the words that follow provide hope and comfort to those still searching for God's grace.

This Book

You may rightfully ask, if I found the Rock on July 4, 1956, why did I live most of my early life struggling to get out of sinking sand? I based most of my life on correcting my behavior rather than seeking the Christ of Calvary. I read that Albert Einstein's wife was once asked if she could understand her husband's theory of relativity. She said she could not, but she understood her husband, and that was more important.

Hebrews 11:3 states, "Through faith we understand." It does not say we will understand everything intellectually, nor does it say we will never have a question. "Through faith," I was fortunate to find the Rock, but finding Him did not solve all my problems. In fact, after I made the commitment of giving my heart and life to Christ, my struggles began on a spiritual level! I continued to make mistakes both big and small, but I always knew that my faith would eventually lead me to a place of spiritual safety.

A personal relationship with Christ begins with a change of heart, repentance. Becoming a new creature does not translate to absolute perfection, and sanctifying grace does not ensure a life free of mistakes. Most of us have read or heard or perhaps seen someone standing on the corner or in a ball stadium holding a sign that reads: John 3:16. It states, "For God so loved the world, that He gave His only begotten Son, that whosoever believeth in Him should not perish, but have everlasting life."

Many of us, maybe most of us, have never read the next verse, John 3:17. It says, "For God sent not His Son into the world to condemn the world; but that the world through Him might be saved."

Two words in this verse have had a penetratingly marvelous influence on me. The first word is *condemn*. Jesus was firm in stating He does not want us to judge or condemn ourselves or others. In truth, He said in Mark 12:31 that we should love others *as* we love ourselves. He is not a condemning God. He taught in Matthew 7:1 and 7:3 to "judge not, that ye be not judged. [. . .] And why beholdest thou the mote that is in thy brother's eye, but considerest not the beam that is in thine own eye?"

I have to admit that most of my life, I used my own hurts to excuse my failures by criticizing others. Would you believe I can never, even once, remember my parents "sitting in the judgment seat of condemnation" toward others? And yet I always felt condemned.

"What will other people think?"

I struggled mightily with that big piece of wood in my own eye.

The second word is *saved*, better translated *salvaged*. An old garage sat next to the slum-area apartment building where I lived when I was in seminary. A guy who lived next door to me rented the garage and purchased an old, beat-up car from the junkyard. Night after night, faithfully and even in the dead of winter, he restored the car. It didn't happen with the snap of his finger. He worked at it! In about a year, the car underwent an amazing transformation.

The Lord God was definitely in my life, but I still had to work at it. It was one of those "grow in grace" things for me. Working your way to heaven is not required nor desired. However, growing in grace is a definite Scriptural stipulation.

I'm not quite sure why many people bristle at the phrase "you must be born again." A newborn Christian is a baby, indeed, growing little by little.

Jesus came not to accuse, pick us out for judgment, or condemn us. He came to this world to fulfill the Father's plan for justice, giving himself as a sacrifice to infuse us with joy, hope, and love. Isn't it strange—we often reside in our own hell of personal condemnation and guilt!

Of course, I learned the hard way that spending time in sinking sand is no way to find the Rock. Feeling sorry for oneself, sinking in sand, may be part of the human condition. However, in the NIV, Hebrews 4:15–16 explains, "For we do not have a high priest who is unable to empathize with our weaknesses, but we have one who has been tempted in every way, just as we are—yet He did not sin. Let us then approach God's throne of grace with confidence, so that we may receive mercy and find grace to help us in our time of need."

When I think of how He came so far from glory
Came to dwell among the lowly such as I
To suffer shame and such disgrace
On Mount Calvary take my place
Then I ask myself this question
Who am I?
Who am I that The King would bleed and die for
Who am I that He would pray not my will, Thine Lord
The answer I may never know
Why He ever loved me so
But to that old rugged cross He'd go
For who am I?
(Rusty Goodman, "Who Am I," 1964)

God is not emotionally remote, and He provides lessons for us in everything, great and small. I have been a slow learner, but I never gave up.

Carole and I exited our room at the Heritage House Resort & Spa on the Mendocino Coast, where the movie *Same Time, Next Year* was filmed (Alan Alda and Ellen Burstyn). Right on the beautiful Pacific Ocean, waves were crashing into huge boulders far below. The sun was shining. Why did I notice a large *Limacus flavus* slug in the parking lot? The night before, it was close to the steps of our room, about thirty feet away—same slug! I knew it was the same one because I could see his slimy trail. He was heading for some foliage on the other side. A slug travels slower than a snail, but he keeps on heading for the goodies—he never gives up!

My friend, you may be slow, but keep on keeping on. *Never give up!* No one but you has your same vision. No one can take your place. Die out to what other people think! The great God of the universe, the Redeemer of your soul, wants to hear from you. Keep praying. Keep praising! God is not a celestial Santa Claus, but you can be assured He answers prayer. I've never read anything in the Bible that requires you to eat cheese with your wine to have peace, so keep at it!

Bad things are going to happen to good people, as Rabbi Harold Kushner wrote. Sinking sand, if you please. I always thought the title of his book was *Why Bad Things Happen to Good People*. Not so. It is *When Bad Things Happen to Good People*. Jesus said in John 16:33, "In the world ye shall have tribulation: but be of good cheer; I have overcome the world."

Through years of suffering and pain, misunderstanding, and what seemed like endless hopelessness, I learned to take my hurt and praise God. God seems to inhabit the praise of His people. Some might say all you need to do is read *The Power of Positive Thinking*. It's a good book, but it won't satisfy. Neither will *Think and Grow Rich*. Like Jesus in Matthew 27:46, you may cry out in agony, "My God, my God, why hast Thou forsaken me?"

Am I saying that faith is of no use or that faith is all you need to mature? Absolutely not! Does time heal? No, it simply helps. Am I saying that positive thinking is of the devil? Not on your life! Are you supposed to walk around with a cloud over your head? You gotta be kidding! Be sour, negative, down in the dumps? No way! But if you think you can do this life thing by yourself without the hand of God, I guarantee that some time or in some way you'll be jerked back to reality with your little positive attitude wrapped around your little positive neck.

You are a child of God. His will and plan is for you and all of us to live, think, behave, give, share, and love as children of the King.

> Oh! to be like Thee, blessed Redeemer,
> This is my constant longing and prayer;
> Gladly I'll forfeit all of earth's treasures,
> Jesus, Thy perfect likeness to wear.
> Oh, to be like Thee! Oh, to be like Thee,
> Blessed Redeemer, pure as Thou art;
> Come in Thy sweetness, come in Thy fullness;
> Stamp Thine own image deep on my heart.
> (Thomas O. Chisholm, "O to Be Like Thee," 1897)

Isn't it ironic that I didn't get out of sinking sand and didn't find my way to the safety of the Solid Rock until I stopped working for the church? I thought church members would be closer, but as stated earlier, in seminary we were taught not to get too close to anyone so as not to show favoritism. Furthermore, I think my home life kept me from getting too close to anyone. I thought friends would be my Rock. I thought Daddy and Mama were my Rock. I thought money would be my Rock, or popularity, or associating with the movers and shakers of Hollywood, politics, and the monied crowd. Peace doesn't work that way! Finding your way from sinking sand onto Solid Rock doesn't work that way.

God gave us His Word as a guide. One of Jesus's first one-on-one discussions comes from when Nicodemus could not wrap his brain around the mystery of a mere human being born again. Jesus said to him in John 3:3, "Except a man be born again, he cannot see the kingdom of God."

What is that? Admittedly, knowing El Shaddai (God Almighty) is a mystery. As Einstein's wife didn't understand the theory of relativity, we don't and never will understand everything about the mystery of godliness, but we know He will reside in the human heart with such forgiveness and love as to create in us a deep hunger like Jesus mentioned in Matthew 5:6, "Blessed are they which do hunger and thirst after righteousness: for they shall be filled."

All problems are not instantly solved. You can't snap your fingers and suddenly be a perfect human being in all respects. Even Peter, after spending time with Jesus for three years, listening to His sermons and instructions, observing His miracles, and hearing His prayers, cut a man's ear off and denied Christ. We aren't promised we will never again make a mistake in judgment. We aren't promised we will never have troubles and trials. We aren't promised we will never, ever have financial issues or fail in business. However, God knows challenges can be a wonderful growth experience!

The Word through the inspired writings of 2 Peter 3:18 NIV challenges us to "grow in the grace and knowledge of our Lord and Savior Jesus Christ."

In so doing, according to Galatians 5:22–23 NIV, the Spirit produces in us "love, joy, peace, forbearance, kindness, goodness, faithfulness, gentleness, and self-control."

I confess with trepidation that the sinking sands of my early life just about destroyed my foundations, but like Micah 7:8, the Lord is a light for me when I fall or sit in the shadow of trouble. As shown in 1 Corinthians 10:1–4, our spiritual ancestors of the Old Testament "were under the cloud, and all passed through the sea; and were all baptized unto Moses in the cloud and in the sea; and did all eat the same spiritual meat; and did all drink the same spiritual drink: for they drank of that spiritual Rock that followed them: and that Rock was Christ."

> On Christ, the Solid Rock, I stand;
> All other ground is sinking sand,
> All other ground is sinking sand.
> (Edward Mote, "My Hope is Built on Nothing Less," 1834)

Defective Foundation

"But you don't understand . . . I tried to save him!"

I was counseling a married couple in the early years of my ministry, and this outburst arose out of marital frustration in response to my question, "Why do you seem to be attracted to needy men?"

I'm not a psychiatrist or even the son of a psychiatrist, but I'm smart enough to know that marrying someone because they have a need is no way to have a successful marriage. A few hours later, her husband arrived for his appointment all cheery and "on the road again." He had all the answers to everything. Although overconfident, this guy made a revealing and remarkable statement when I asked him what attracted him to his wife.

I may have been using the Rogerian technique, allowing the client to come to their own conclusion.

After a short pause, he said, "You know, I think I get off on the power thing."

I asked what that meant to him.

He responded, "I guess it's a challenge to see if I can conquer women, all kinds and shapes." He laughed.

My astute analysis and illustrious counseling did not keep this marriage from a bad ending.

Pulling a woman through the dirt by her hair might have been the method Neanderthal men used, but in civilized society, it "ain't a-gonna work." When she finally recovers her senses, the conquering man will suddenly know how much power she has. The seduction game ends badly because it's a game. And, for the woman, trying to change him or "save" him is a form of seduction and becomes a conqueror's delight. At first blush, she may seem like a weak damsel in distress, easy prey for conquering, but . . .

You can't be a simpleton by dismissively calling it a Mars and Venus conflict. When Jesus said to "Love the Lord thy God," and added, "Love thy neighbor as thyself," you could change the word *neighbor* to *wife* or *husband*.

St. Paul put it this way in Ephesians 5:22 and 5:25. "Husbands, love your wives, even as Christ also loved the church, and gave himself for it." To the wife, he says, "Wives, submit yourselves unto your own husbands, as unto the Lord." This thing called marriage must be a joint effort!

In my opinion, the modern-day movement to create chaos in America has interjected its filthy fingers into our culture and political system through the feminist philosophy of dividing and promoting gender-based distinctions. Marriage should not be based on me, myself, and I, nor should it be solely based on sexual attraction as our culture seems to define it. Perhaps this philosophy is why we have more than a 50 percent divorce rate. I know of one woman who has been married more than eight times (that I know of). It's not unusual to meet men who have had multiple marriages as well, and our degradative culture has invaded the Christian community to the point where divorce is brushed off like dandruff from our shoulders.

The foundations are defective. Jesus gave the proper example when He took the towel, even though He was God Almighty and given all power by the Father. He knelt before His disciples and washed their feet.

Embarrassingly so, my first marriage exposed my own cracked and marred foundation.

Rules

Rules are not my thing because they remind me of old Mrs. McAfee, one of my third-grade teachers. She was big on rules! The seven rules for highly effective people, or rules for thinking "possibility thoughts," are on a different level from the spiritual. Although Jesus did not denounce the commandments of the prophets and others, His plan for us is to surrender to the saving grace and powerful plan of God's loving forgiveness. It may be a mystery, but as St. Paul wrote in 1 Corinthians 15:51 and 54–57, "Behold, I shew you a mystery; we shall not all sleep, but we shall all be changed [. . .]. So when this corruptible shall have put on incorruption, and this mortal shall have put on immortality, then shall be brought to pass the saying that is written, Death is swallowed up in victory. O death, where is thy sting? O grave, where is thy victory? The sting of death is sin; and the strength of sin is the law. But thanks be to God, which giveth us the victory through our Lord Jesus Christ."

After many decades of life, I've learned a few bits of wisdom that have helped me and I hope will help others. Call them rules, if you like, or not. Here are my suggestions for living a better life.

Keep on keeping on.

Take charge.

Be kind even when you don't feel like it.

Honor your parents, regardless.

Take time to worship.

Think before you act.

Remember that people will always act like people.

Love unconditionally or change without regret.

Surrender to God's plan.

Covet personal integrity.

Who Would Have Thought?

While sitting in a ministers' meeting of various denominations back in the 1960s, a vociferous pastor jumped to his feet and shouted a well-known four-letter word. I'm not sure why, but I guess he wanted to let everyone know that churches need not be what we had always thought them to be.

During that same meeting, the sharpest clashes centered on ecumenism, church unity, ordaining women, and homosexuality. In the sixties!

Harry Golden, editor of the *Carolina Israelite*, was skeptical of all churches. This Jewish editor was quoted in *Life Magazine* as saying, "If I were faced today with the decision my ancestors faced [. . .] 'become a Christian or die,' I would pick a church fast. There is nothing to offend me in the modern church. The minister gives a talk on juvenile delinquency one week, reviews a movie the next week, then everyone goes downstairs and plays bingo. The first part of a church they build nowadays is the kitchen. Five hundred years from now, people will dig up these churches, find the steam tables, and wonder what kind of sacrifices we performed."

I read of a large church in a metropolitan area embarking on a building program. The church was of Georgian style. The question arose about what to put on top of the steeple. With no argument from anyone, they decided not to place a cross on top, but a weather vane, because it was more in keeping with the architectural style. And so the church in that community holds aloft the symbol of its gospel, not a cross or spire, but a weather vane that blows like the tumbling tumbleweed.

I would much rather stay with basic Christian theology.

In John 14:6, Christ is "the way, the truth, and the life."

In Titus 2:14, Christ "gave himself for us, that He might redeem us from all iniquity, and purify unto himself a peculiar people, zealous of good works."

In Hebrews 2:9, Christ "was made a little lower than the angels for the suffering of death, crowned with glory and honor; that He by the grace of God should taste death for every man."

In Hebrews 4:15, Christ "was in all points tempted like as we are, yet without sin."

In Hebrews 13:12, Christ, "that He might sanctify the people with His own blood, suffered without the gate."

In Hebrews 12:2, Christ is "the author and finisher of our faith; who for the joy that was set before Him endured the cross, despising the shame, and is set down at the right hand of the throne of God."

In Hebrews 9:28, Christ "once offered to bear the sins of many; and unto them that look for Him shall He appear the second time without sin unto salvation."

In 1 Corinthians 1:18, the biblical preaching of the cross "is to them that perish foolishness; but unto us which are saved it is the power of God." In Acts 4:10, Peter used "Jesus Christ of Nazareth, whom ye crucified" as his sermon topic. And again, Peter, looking toward the cross that dripped with sinless blood, wrote in 1 Peter 2:24, "Who His own self bare our sins in His own body on the tree, that we, being dead to sins, should live unto righteousness: by whose stripes ye were healed."

Samuel Zwemer, an American missionary born in the 1800s, said in his book *The Glory of the Cross* that "the longest shadow in the world is the shadow of the cross." That shadow zigzagged its way into the temple and ripped the veil from top to bottom. It stretched its fingers into the dark recesses of death's grave and liberated the dead. Its luminous glow reached into the upper room where He entered, "the doors being shut," showing them His hands, His side, and His feet. It fell across Mount Olivet as the disciples gazed into heaven. It climbed the stairs once more to that upper room and burst upon the faithful few like peals of thunder and tongues of fire until the weak in faith became strong and the weary and despondent spoke with certainty.

The shadow of the cross wound its way up the black tower of an Augustinian monastery in Wittenberg to the heart of a German-born monk, and the Reformation was born. Then it went on to the heart of a young Anglican clergyman on May 24, 1738, and the Methodist Revival influenced the world. But in 1956, that same shadow lay across the state of New Mexico, settled down on an old-fashioned youth camp, and made real for me the crimson cash payment of His precious blood until I sang:

I stand amazed in the presence
Of Jesus, the Nazarene,
And wonder how He could love me,
A sinner, condemned, unclean.
(Charles H. Gabriel, "My Savior's Love," 1905)

While visiting the Vatican's Sistine Chapel in 1985, I learned of Michelangelo going to a public auction where artists were bidding on marble pieces for their work, hoping for a handsome return. An old, dirty piece of marble lay on the side; no one seemed interested in it. At the end of the auction, Michelangelo made a low bid, purchasing the piece of marble no one wanted.

"Why would you want an ugly, dirty, unwanted piece of marble?" people nearby asked him.

He answered, "There's an angel in there and I must set it free."

O the glory of His presence!

I cannot tell thee whence it came
This peace within my breast;
But this I know, there fills my soul
A strange and tranquil rest.
There's a deep, settled peace in my soul,
There's a deep, settled peace in my soul,
Tho' the billows of sin near me roll,
He abides, Christ abides.
(John S. Brown, "Hidden Peace," 1899)

Out of Bondage

I presume you would like to have eternal life. Here's how.

Recognize the truth of what Jesus said in John 3:3, "Verily, verily, I say unto thee, Except a man be born again, he cannot see the kingdom of God." Acts 4:12 says, "Neither is there salvation in any other: for there is none other name under heaven given among men, whereby we must be saved."

Based on John 3:16–17, believe that God loves you, gave His Son for you, and didn't come to judge you.

Believe that you have a problem called sin! And sin causes eternal death and separation from God. Romans 6:23 says, "For the wages of sin is death; but the gift of God is eternal life through Jesus Christ our Lord." Accept and repent of this fact—you are a sinner. You can't buy your way in. You can't earn your way in.

Believe 1 Corinthians 15:3–4, which says, "Christ died for our sins according to the scriptures; and that He was buried, and that He rose again the third day according to the scriptures." Believe by faith that although you are a sinner, Christ died for you.

Confess with great sorrow that you are willing to give up a sinful life. That's called repentance! Surrender! Know that 1 John 1:9 says, "If we confess our sins, He is faithful and just to forgive us our sins, and to cleanse us from all unrighteousness."

You will be reunited with God through Christ, as described in Revelation 3:20, "Behold, I stand at the door, and knock: if any man hear my voice, and open the door, I will come in to him, and will sup with him, and he with me."

Out of my bondage, sorrow, and night,
Jesus, I come, Jesus, I come;
Into Thy freedom, gladness, and light,
Jesus, I come to Thee.
Out of my sickness into Thy health,
Out of my want and into Thy wealth,
Out of my sin and into Thyself,
Jesus, I come to Thee.
Out of my shameful failure and loss,
Jesus, I come, Jesus, I come;
Into the glorious gain of Thy cross,
Jesus, I come to Thee.
Out of earth's sorrows into Thy balm,
Out of life's storms and into Thy calm,
Out of distress to jubilant psalm,
Jesus, I come to Thee.
(William T. Sleeper, "Out of My Bondage, Sorrow, and Night,"
1887)

The Shoe Is Perfect

Daddy took my horse, Smokey, to the blacksmith to get new shoes. I was about seven years old in 1945. With wide eyes, I watched as the blacksmith put iron in the fire. He left it there until it got red-hot. Then he pulled it out with a big, long tool and placed it on the anvil—glowing! He beat and banged on it until sparks flew! Because the iron was so hot, it was kinda soft. He hammered it, twisting it into a horseshoe. He already knew Smokey's size, I guess. He put it in the water, and it sizzled. He made four of them. Smokey stood watching. When the blacksmith put them on Smokey, both he and the horse seemed happy.

I thought this was gonna be really bad with all the fire, noise, and beating. Maybe Smokey did, too. But Daddy knew exactly who to go to for brand-new shoes. Daddy loved Smokey, and so did I. In a way, I think the blacksmith did, too. Neither Daddy nor the blacksmith would dare hurt Smokey. Lessons I learned:

1. God *does not* cause us to suffer. He works through our circumstances.
2. He uses many events and crises to make our lives better.
3. He is *love*; He knows just the right things to do to make the "shoe" fit.
4. He perfectly understands things may look scary, but the shoes He puts on us will protect us when we run over rough ground.

Romans 8:28 says, "And we know that all things work together for good to them that love God, to them who are the called according to His purpose."

Why People Hurt

I had my pastoral hat on. (I was so young.) Tears of confusion poured from her eyes. She was a relatively new Christian. Her little son had just died, and her husband was angry. He was mad at her, God, and everyone! In addition, they were in debt, head over heels.

With pleading eyes, she said, "But I thought Jesus was supposed to help us. Where is God when you need Him?"

I was thinking, *Does she think God caused this? Does she think God allowed this? Did I teach her this?*

Maybe I should have said, "Well, we live in an evil world."

Both she and her husband would have thrown me out of the house . . . and he was a big guy.

At this point, I don't think quoting the Bible would have helped. In the NIV, John 16:33 says, "In this world you will have trouble. But take heart! I have overcome the world." John spoke the truth.

Nevertheless, this woman had a sincere question. She wouldn't have accepted a Scriptural exegesis. A saccharine-sweet brush-off wouldn't do from a twenty-seven-year-old preacher. She was in emotional and spiritual pain!

When someone has a terrible automobile accident and is lying in the middle of the road, their blood everywhere, a doctor would not give them a classroom lecture on trauma. Sorry, Charlie. It's not the right time or place. Furthermore, the pain would be too excruciating. I was trying to figure out why people hurt and how to work through their trauma. I've come up with these seven ways to think about it.

Number one, start *before* the injury and pain, before the heartache, before the discouragement or disappointment, before the treason or lies, before the uncertainty or questions. The relationship we have with Christ Jesus through the power of the Holy Spirit and a voracious hunger for His Word, the Bible, our spiritual road map—is our protection and peace. Few people consume the Word of God on a daily basis, and even fewer memorize it.

Jesus said in John 10:14, "I am the good shepherd, and know my sheep, and am known of mine." Romans 5:8–9 says, "But God commendeth His love toward us, in that, while we were yet sinners, Christ died for us. Much more then, being now justified by His blood, we shall be saved from wrath through Him." In 2 Timothy 1:7, St. Paul wrote, "For God hath not given us the spirit of fear; but of power, and of love, and of a sound mind."

Number two, the Rorschach test was designed to help the psychologist delve deep into the subject's thinking, diagnosing their mental state. Excluding destructive behavior, when people try to diagnose how or why human beings suffer—usually by blaming God—they only create more suffering through hate, anger, and despondency. When suffering through heartaches, should we blame God or perhaps go to a street-side mind reader?

Trust me on this, things will happen in your life for which you have no answer—none. You can read books about why bad things happen to good people, and it may bring a little comfort, somewhat like rubbing lidocaine on a sore tooth, but when God works with us through our hurt, He goes to the heart of the matter. Count on this— He does not cause human suffering, but in many cases, He will pick up the pieces left along the way. He welcomes us as we fall helplessly into His bosom. Even Jesus, who was God in the flesh, had terrible feelings of hopelessness. Even in His soul's agony, He cried in Matthew 27:46, "My God, my God, why hast Thou forsaken me?"

Number three, over and over throughout the Bible, the Lord challenges us by saying, "Do not be afraid." When the disciples were about to drown, Jesus said, "Do not be afraid."

When a celestial being appeared before the shepherds, it scared the living daylights out of them. Think of it—thousands of angels spread across the sky, singing. I would be scared, too. An angel said to them, "Do not be afraid."

In the NIV, Revelation 2:10 indicates that Satan causes suffering. It says, "Do not be afraid of what you are about to suffer. I tell you, the devil will put some of you in prison to test you, and you will suffer [. . .]. Be faithful, even to the point of death, and I will give you life as your victor's crown."

Number four, how about those three hanging on crosses? Two of them were criminals. The One in the center was God, pure and holy, who took upon himself flesh and bone. In his pain and suffering, one of the thieves railed at Jesus and mockingly said in Luke 23:39, "If Thou be Christ, save Thyself and us."

Jesus never shouted back condemnation to the bitter thief.

Number five, sometimes the pain we feel is because we don't know what to do. It's as though there is no answer. We're hopeless.

"What do I do now? Is there no one to help me?"

In Acts 16:25–26, Paul and Silas sat in a dungeon and "prayed and sang praises unto God, and [. . .] suddenly there was a great earthquake, so that the foundations of the prison were shaken: and immediately all the doors were opened, and every one's bands were loosed." Strange as it may seem, when our hurt is the most caustic, our praises should be the most abundant.

Number six, rather than dealing with the *why* of suffering, the key is to deal with the solution. The solution is to *praise* Him. Praising shows trust!

Number seven, and again, praise Him!

Praise Him! Praise Him! Jesus, our blessed Redeemer!
Sing, O earth, His wonderful love proclaim!

Hail Him! Hail Him! Highest archangels in glory,
Strength and honor give to His holy name!
Like a shepherd, Jesus will guard His children;
In His arms He carries them all day long:
Praise Him! Praise Him! Tell of His excellent greatness!
Praise Him! Praise Him! Ever in joyful song!
(Fanny Crosby, "Praise Him! Praise Him!" 1869)

The Answer

Do you remember the TV situation comedy *Gomer Pyle: USMC* that ran from 1964 to 1969? Gomer's famous statement was, "Surprise! Surprise!" Permit me to surprise you. There are some things I just don't know! And neither do you.

When I walk into my garage, get into my car, and turn the key, I don't really know with certainty if the car will start. By faith, I believe it will. If it doesn't, I call AAA. In my greatest pain, I learned to call on the Comforter, the Holy Spirit, and amazingly, He enlightens my day. When I drive down the street, I believe it will be a safe journey, and seldom do I think about it. Faith! I make plans for tomorrow, but I don't know if I'll make it through the night. It never enters my mind. Faith! I pray. I confess. I give thanks. I make supplications. I surrender. My soul is filled with glory!

I have so many questions about life and why people suffer. Why this, and why that? I don't know why my heart hurts. Why did things happen the way they did? Will I ever make it? Where is God when I suffer? You've been in that place, haven't you? The key to healing is to "trust and obey," as in John H. Sammis's 1887 hymn, "for there's no other way to be happy in Jesus, but to trust and obey."

Disastrous things happen in life. You may have unsolvable marriage problems. Your business may be on the verge of bankruptcy. You coughed tea through your nose at a formal banquet with your employer. You stubbed your toe on the bed frame. You or a family member developed a devastating health crisis. Why, oh Lord, why?

The natural response to bad things is to say, "God, if you love me, why did you let this happen?" Blame, blame, blame! Is that any way to express love?

Surprise! We don't need to know everything. What we need to know is the Comforter. He is the One in charge, and He knows exactly the answer. He is the Spirit of God. You can't grasp Him. You can't weigh Him. Like a soft breeze on your face, you can't see Him, but you know He is there. He is not an *it*. He is the third person of the Holy Trinity. He has the power to work things out for our good and His glory!

How does this work? Colossians 2:11–15 and 18–23 MSG explains it this way:

> Entering into this fullness is not something you figure out or achieve. It's not a matter of being circumcised or keeping a long list of laws. No, you're already *in*—insiders—not through some secretive initiation rite but rather through what Christ has already gone through for you, destroying the power of sin. If it's an initiation ritual you're after, you've already been through it by submitting to baptism. Going under the water was a burial of your old life; coming up out of it was a resurrection, God raising you from the dead as He did Christ. When you were stuck in your old sin-dead life, you were incapable of responding to God. God brought you alive—right along with Christ! Think of it! All sins forgiven, the slate wiped clean, that old arrest warrant canceled and nailed to Christ's cross. He stripped all the spiritual tyrants in the universe of their sham authority at the Cross and marched them naked through the streets.
>
> Don't tolerate people who try to run your life, ordering you to bow and scrape, insisting that you join their obsession with angels and that you seek out visions. They're a lot of hot air, that's all they are. They're completely out of touch with the source of life, Christ, who puts us together in one piece, whose very breath and blood flow through us. He is the Head and we are the body. We can grow up healthy in God only as He nourishes us.
>
> So, then, if with Christ you've put all that pretentious and infantile religion behind you, why do you let yourselves be bullied by it? "Don't touch this! Don't taste that! Don't go near this!" Do you think things

that are here today and gone tomorrow are worth that kind of attention? Such things sound impressive if said in a deep enough voice. They even give the illusion of being pious and humble and ascetic. But they're just another way of showing off, making yourselves look important.

In my book *Write It on My Heart,* some of my readers were puzzled about the last chapter on peace. I think it was because I used the word *essence!* I wrote:

Eureka! I've got the answer. It suddenly dawned on me. Essence! We want stuff now, no waiting in line, no diversions, no excuses, no problems, no sorrow, no worry, no hurt, no pain, no misunderstanding, no suffering, no stink, no bum-rap, and no complaints! It ain't a-gonna happen on this earth! [. . .]

So make up your mind. If you are going to follow the Master, give it up! Surrender! There is a peace that passes all understanding. It goes far beyond your pain. It goes far beyond your sorrow. If you want that liberating release from misunderstanding, blame, and God-questioning hurt, you just gotta make up your mind to be a slave of the *one* who is saving you for eternity. That's the *essence* of it all!

18

What's Your Story?

Everyone has a story. There are givers and there are takers, the give-uppers and the overcomers. There are those who suffered great tragedy or committed a great sin, but through their tears and broken hearts, they held on just one more hour. At the end of their lives, God will speak to them like He did in Matthew 25:23 to the man who had been a good steward of his talents, "Well done, good and faithful servant; thou hast been faithful over a few things, I will make thee ruler over many things: enter thou into the joy of thy lord."

God told Moses to lead, but he was a stutterer and had killed a guy. David was just a kid when he became a hero. But as king, he let his hormones get the best of him and had the husband of Bathsheba, the object of his affection, killed. Hosea, the prophet, married a prostitute. Peter cut a guy's ear off. Paul went around killing Christians.

"Oh, but that was a long time ago and in the Bible to boot," you say. Nevertheless, those were their stories. What's yours?

I'm not free to reveal a name, but I knew a prince of a man, a friend of my dad, who was born of a prostitute under a bridge in the early 1900s before a system was in place to take care of him. Some Christian people, members of a little clapboard church, found him when he was six years of age and took him to Sunday school. He gave his heart to

Christ. They nurtured him along the way. He grew up, went to a Christian college with no money, could not pay tuition, and slept on the lawn for three days. The college authorities had compassion and gave him a job as a plumber; he graduated and became a leader in his church denomination.

So what is your story?

> Keep holding on, just one more hour
> May bring to thee the promised pow'r;
> Keep holding on, thy Lord doth care,
> He'll not forget to answer prayer.
> Keep holding on, keep holding on,
> The victory will soon be won;
> The longest day will soon be gone,
> Keep holding on, keep holding on.
> Keep holding on, Christ knows thy need,
> He doth the hungry sparrows feed;
> Keep holding on, He'll hear thy cry,
> Thy Lord is watching from on high.
> (William C. Poole, "Keep Holding On," 1913)

Humpty Dumpty

> All the king's horses and all the king's men
> couldn't put Humpty together again.
>
> — SAMUEL ARNOLD, *JUVENILE AMUSEMENTS*,
> 1797

You may feel irreparably broken.

Your life may be a wreck.

You may feel desperately hopeless.

The evil one is trying every trick in his book to discourage you, to make you lose faith.

Don't fall for it. He's a deceiver.

On the other hand, the great God of heaven, Creator, Comforter, Savior, El Shaddai, is the Son of Righteousness.

He's the King of Glory.

The firmament shows His handiwork.

He made himself known in the burning bush.

He gave strength to David.

He loved when early man didn't know what love was.

He called himself in Exodus 3:14, "I Am That I Am."

He's enduringly strong.

He's eternally gracious.

He's the miracle of ages.

He's the friend of sinners.

He's the Great Physician.

He's imperially powerful.

He's impartially merciful.

He's my friend!

He's your friend.

He makes a way when there is none.

The NIV in Matthew 12:20–21 declares, "A bruised reed He will not break, and a smoldering wick He will not snuff out, till He has brought justice through to victory. In His name the nations will put their hope."

Jesus said in Matthew 28:20, "I am with you always, to the very end of the age."

The Church in the Age of Relativism

Next door to my daughter's apartment is a prominent downtown church, a rather large building. She invited me to go with her to explore the possibility of making it her church home. No one greeted us, but a sign stood there, notifying attendees to help themselves to the daily program.

After being seated, I opened the program. The title of the service was "Honoring Great American Feminists"—Bella Abzug, Hillary Clinton, Angela Davis, Betty Friedan, Oprah Winfrey, Gloria Steinem, and a few names I didn't recognize. The music consisted of the organ playing, no congregational singing. The pastor reminded us of a few community activities and then directed those gathered to refer to the program. He gave us the title of his speech: "The Day of the Woman." So far, we'd heard nothing about God, Jesus, the Holy Spirit, the Nicene Creed, Abraham, Samson and Delilah, or the virgin Mary, nor did the preacher use a Scriptural basis, not even Proverbs 31:10–31.

We had enough, so we left, and a few others did the same. If I'm not mistaken, we thought we would hear something about Jesus. No way, Jose!

Relativism is the philosophy that truth depends upon only each individual's beliefs and experiences. In plain English, it means truth is not absolute! In Shakespeare's *Hamlet*, Hamlet declares to Rosencrantz, "For there is nothing either good or bad, but thinking makes it so." There you have it. There is no truth; truth is only what you make it through your life experiences.

According to relativism, fundamental truth does not exist. Everything is nuanced. To be up-to-date and appeal to the younger crowd, the hip "speecher" must make the Bible relevant to today's way of thinking, "a living, breathing" document that flows with what's culturally acceptable rather than Scripturally sound. Forget theology. Forget the Bible. Forget thees and thous. OK? Some will say, "It's better to get them through the doors of the church than to force them to stay at the nightclub!"

Activities, music, and customs have always changed with the times. No problem so far. But wait a minute—wait a minute. It has only been in the last fifty to sixty years that the Christian beliefs taught in the Nicene Creed have been deleted from our pulpits. Consequently, most of the younger crowd today know nothing about the Trinity or heaven or hell or sin. They may know a little about the niceties of accepting Jesus as their personal Savior (as long as it doesn't interrupt their lifestyle), but please don't encourage them to repent or cry over Calvary or the blood. They want cheap grace. If you preach too strongly about repentance and confession of sins, they'll just go to another church. They want to hear things that lift them up and make them feel good.

Lord knows how we need to hear some good stuff with all the bad things we see on TV news, and besides, isn't there only one God anyway? Why can't we be like Ancient Greece with many gods? Or the Hindus? Since Christian theology and the Christian belief system have been thrown out the window, we can say that the golden calf, Allah, Thor, Zeus, Jesus, and whoever are all gods.

Trinity? "Forget it. I can't explain it anyway."

Heaven? "Do you mean aliens in spaceships? UFOs?"

Repentance? "Well, I'm sorry about a lot of things."

Praying? "OMG, yes. I pray all the time."

Living a holy life? "You gotta be kidding. I'm no monk. And nobody's perfect."

In 2 Timothy 4:3–5 MSG, Paul writes, "You're going to find that there will be times when people will have no stomach for solid teaching, but will fill up on spiritual junk food—catchy opinions that tickle their fancy. They'll turn their backs on truth and chase mirages. But you—keep your eye on what you're doing; accept the hard times along with the good; keep the Message alive; do a thorough job as God's servant."

What is a true church? Is Jesus's church an organization, an architecturally ornate building, a basketball arena, or an auditorium filled with happy-happy people listening to the latest rock music and a "speecher" who stands on stage with one hand in the pocket of his torn jeans, wearing sneakers while he makes everyone laugh? Is it a place where you can live like the devil all week long and come to "The Place" or "The Center" or "The Table" on Sunday, get out early for lunch, and head for the beach? Is a great church one that attracts the most people?

What about the music? Does it truly bring out praises to God, or does it simply tickle your fancy? Do you sing, "I love you. I love you. I'm gonna move you. I love you. I love you. I'm gonna groove wit'chew." (Be sure to sing it eleven times.) Or is it:

How firm a foundation, ye saints of the Lord.
Is laid for your faith in God's excellent Word!
What more can be said than to you God hath said,
To you who for refuge to Jesus have fled?
(John Rippon, "How Firm a Foundation," 1787)

God's holy place of worship is, according to the Word of God in Acts 4:33 NLT, a gathering of those who testify "powerfully to the resurrection of the Lord Jesus, and God's great blessing was upon them all."

In the early church, the power of the Holy Spirit worked through believers. They weren't trying to be relevant. They weren't trying to force the Word into their cultural box. They weren't trying to be a late-night venue for comedians. It was so holy that when a man and his wife lied, God struck them dead! I fear many churches today are too busy counting nickels and noses to be filled with the Holy Spirit, to testify powerfully, and to be a great blessing!

Feeling Hopeless?

Is it because you think you should be punished?

In the Philippines, just before Easter, men will whip and beat themselves until they are bloodied almost to death. Some have been known to try crucifixion. This is self-flagellation—striking yourself with a whip as punishment in a religious ritual.

A guy in south Texas once said to me, "Man, I've really been an idiot."

He had no church background. He didn't understand "churchy" language. He really didn't even know what sin was. All he knew was that because of his behavior, he had almost ruined his life. He felt hopeless because he thought he needed punishment.

I told him about Jesus, the Savior, but when I tried to approach the need for his salvation, he kept coming back to how big of an idiot he was and how he needed to be "smacked upside da hayud." (Texas slanguage.) He was mentally and emotionally broken. He thought his only answer to peace was self-flagellation.

You may think you have been an idiot. It may seem as though there is no hope. It may look like God's forgiveness is too easy—your sin is too great, and your only hope is to have your legs broken.

God's answer through Christ is, "Don't worry!" Worry, self-punishment, fear, doubt, hopelessness, and anxiety are not the answer to idiocy and sin!

Ephesians 2:1–6 MSG explains it this way:

It wasn't so long ago that you were mired in that old stagnant life of
sin. You let the world, which doesn't know the first thing about living,
tell you how to live. You filled your lungs with polluted unbelief, and
then exhaled disobedience. We all did it, all of us doing what we felt
like doing, when we felt like doing it, all of us in the same boat. It's a
wonder God didn't lose His temper and do away with the whole lot of
us. Instead, immense in mercy and with an incredible love, He
embraced us. He took our sin-dead lives and made us alive in Christ.
He did all this on His own, with no help from us! Then He picked us
up and set us down in highest heaven in company with Jesus, our
Messiah.

> Near the cross, a trembling soul,
> Love and mercy found me;
> There the Bright and Morning Star
> Shed His beams around me.
> Near the cross! I'll watch and wait,
> Hoping, trusting ever;
> Till I reach the golden strand,
> Just beyond the river.
> In the cross, in the cross
> Be my glory ever,
> Till my ransomed soul shall find
> Rest beyond the river.
> (Fanny Crosby, "Jesus, Keep Me Near the Cross," 1869)

Strain a Gnat

I don't care about most of the things those preachers on TV do. For
instance, I really don't care if the earth was formed six thousand or ten
billion years ago. I don't think the Lord God inspired the Bible to be a
book of irrefutable science. If it was important for us to know exactly
when and how the earth was formed, He would have made it abundantly clear.

If Jesus had wanted us to know the exact date of His second coming, He would have told us. And yet I have heard a few TV guys and others laboriously trying to find in Scripture and signs in the sky when we will see Jesus coming. I'm ready! Are you? Maybe those speeching and preaching entertainers are too busy raising money for their $50 million jet planes to do as 2 Timothy 4:2 NIV says and "preach the word; be prepared in season and out of season; correct, rebuke, and encourage—with great patience and careful instruction."

I heard a guy on TV say we are going to be in heaven exactly the way we are on earth but without the limitations. *Reeeally?*

As for me, I don't want to be like I am now. I like myself, kinda, but I'm not a narcissist. Being free of limitations may be great, but I would need to strain at a gnat and swallow a camel to find anything like that in the Bible. I'll guarantee you, when Jesus comes—whenever that may be—and He introduces me to my heavenly body:

> There'll be singing, there'll be shouting
> When the saints come marching home,
> In Jerusalem, in Jerusalem,
> Waving palms with loud hosannas
> As the King shall take His throne,
> In the new Jerusalem.
> (C. B. Widmeyer, "In the New Jerusalem," 1939)

Much of that preaching is designed to either raise money or scare the living daylights out of people. My heart and life are ready. I love the Savior, and He loves me, and His saving grace makes me unbelievably happy.

> Whenever I am tempted, whenever clouds arise,
> When songs give place to sighing, when hope within me dies,
> I draw the closer to Him, from care He sets me free;
> His eye is on the sparrow, and I know He watches me;
> His eye is on the sparrow, and I know He watches me.
> I sing because I'm happy,
> I sing because I'm free,

For His eye is on the sparrow,
And I know He watches me.
(Civilla D. Martin, "His Eye is on the Sparrow," 1905)

Dancing through the Tulips

If all you need to do is think positive thoughts, eat broccoli, associate with happy people, make a ton of money, listen to uplifting speeches, live in an upper-class part of town, read possibility books, and plant your "seed money" with some TV preacher in the hope of being healthy, wealthy, and wise (and help him buy his new jet airplane), why, then, my dear friend—

Do You Need God?

I agree with those who say it is not necessary to have God in your life to be rich and happy-happy! Believe it or not, lots of money may be and could be satisfying . . . to a degree. Reading positive books and attending motivational seminar-like sermons can be inspiring. You can live next door to a family with seven beautiful kids, enjoy a twelve-thousand-square-foot home, make a ton of money, be happy as you drive up in your European car to the portico of a prominent church with thousands of attendees . . . and still be lost!

As Jesus said in Mark 8:36, "For what shall it profit a man, if he shall gain the whole world, and lose his own soul?"

You and I need God to give us liberty in our inner self. All of us have probably known or heard of someone who had everything this world could give and yet were lost in their soul. They spent their time with money, fame, and fortune—just before they committed suicide! Many of those happy-happy people turn to alcohol, drugs, and prostitutes. Hello out there!

Obviously, many people live their entire life dancing through the tulips. You may be one of those. Congratulations. You may never need God to help you live an upper-class life.

But what happens thereafter . . . ?

In John 6:35 NIV, Jesus said, "I am the bread of life. Whoever comes to me will never go hungry, and whoever believes in me will never be thirsty."

All that I need He will always be
All that I need till His face I see
All that I need thro' eternity
Jesus is all I need.
(James Rowe, "Jesus Is All I Need," 1927)

Winter

It's 3:00 a.m. Cold. Foggy. George H. W. Bush is gone at ninety-four. My good friend Reverend Les Shelton passed away at seventy-eight. My friend Danny Steele, with whom I traveled for four years in the Collegiate Quartet, passed away, as did Steve Brown. It's winter.

Long ago, Willie Nelson wrote, "Ain't it funny how time slips away." Yes, it's winter. It caught me off guard—before I knew what was happening. It makes no difference that Willie also wrote, "I'd trade all my tomorrows for just one yesterday," because my future is as bright as the promises of God. Yes, part of my past was painful. If I had to do it over, I would change a few things. I shoulda, coulda, woulda. Isn't that the case with most of us?

But now the days are short,
I'm in the [winter] of the year
And now I think of my life as vintage wine
From fine old kegs
From the brim to the dregs,
And it poured sweet and clear
It was a very good year.
(Ervin Drake, "It Was a Very Good Year," 1961)

Forgetting the past, you can

Take the world, but give me Jesus;
In His cross my trust shall be,

191

Till, with clearer, brighter vision,
Face to face my Lord I see.
(Fanny Crosby, "Take the World, but Give Me Jesus," 1879)

It's still winter. It was just yesterday—it seems like yesterday—I
was so immature, in high school, college, embarking in a fragile canoe
called life. I held my son in loving arms as he looked at me with blue
eyes.

I said to him, "My son, I love you so much."

He looked at me as though he answered, "I love you, too."

Time caught me. Where did the years go?

And then in El Paso, living on a dirt road in an adobe house two
miles from Juarez, Mexico, my precious daughter caught her first
breath in Providence Hospital, laboring as though she would die with
Hyaline membrane disease. I couldn't hold or touch her for nine days.
We had no money to pay for hospital care. Would she be left to die?
Would it be winter in springtime? I loved her and carefully cared
for her.

The grunt work as a small-church pastor chased me, but like a
breath of fresh air in springtime, hope found me in the midst of my
slog. Oh my, my, yes!

I knew I was blood-bought. And yes, the Rock had a plan!

Like the sunshine after rain, Like the rest that follows pain,
Like a hope returned again, Is the peace that Jesus gives.
(Haldor Lillenas, "The Peace that Jesus Gives," 1917)

Springtime came in the form of an addition to my son and daughter. Carole brought her two amazing little guys, six and three, some
forty years ago, joining us to make a family unit of six. It was spring!

Hopes and dreams are lit anew.

Yet in a way, it seems like eons ago, and I wonder where all the years have gone. I know I lived them all. I have glimpses of how it was back then and of all my hopes and dreams. But here it is . . . the winter of my life, and it caught me by surprise. How did I get here so fast? Where did the years go? What happened to my youth?

I well remember seeing older people through the years and thinking that those old people were years away from me and that winter was so far off. I could not fathom it or imagine what it would be like.

But here it is. My friends are retired and gray. They move slower, and I see older people now. Some are in better and some worse shape than I, but I see a change. They're not like the people I remember who were young and vibrant . . . like me, their age is showing, and we are now *those older folks* we used to see and never thought we'd be.

Each day now, finding my way to the shower takes a concerted effort. Taking a nap is not a treat anymore; it's mandatory, because if I don't of my own free will, I fall asleep wherever I sit!

And so now I enter this new season of my life unprepared for all the aches and pains and the loss of strength and ability to do things I wish I had done but never did!

Yes, I have regrets. I'm not perfect. I wish I hadn't done some things . . . and I wish I *had* done others, but indeed, I'm happy to have done many things. It's all in a lifetime.

If you're not in your winter yet, let me remind you, it will be here faster than you think. Whatever you would like to accomplish in your life, please do it quickly! Don't put things off too long! Life goes by quickly. Do what you can today, as you can never be sure whether this is your last winter or not! You have no promise you will see all the seasons of your life.

Squeeze the sweet juice of today. Say all the things you want your loved ones to remember, and, like Hank Cochran said, "make the world go away."

These are the best days of my life! As in Psalm 23 NIV, the Rock led me through the "valley of the shadow of death" and taught me not to fear even when I was scared out of my mind. He prepared "a table before me in the presence of my enemies," and anointed "my [. . .] head with oil." He leads me in the path of righteousness for His name's sake, saying in John 14:27 NLT, "I am leaving you with a gift— peace of mind and heart. And the peace I give is a gift the world cannot give. So don't be troubled or afraid."

> Rock of Ages, cleft for me,
> Let me hide myself in Thee;
> Let the water and the blood,
> From Thy wounded side which flowed,
> Be of sin the double cure,
> Save from wrath and make me pure.
> (Augustus M. Toplady, "Rock of Ages," 1775)